U.S.A.
Immigration
Guide

INCLUDING THE NEW RULES FOR THE
IMMIGRATION ACT OF 1990

with

New Opportunities for
Investor Permanent Residency and
Non–Immigrant Visas

By Ramon Carrion
Attorney at Law

Admitted to practice in Florida and New Jersey

78476

SPHINX PUBLISHING
Sphinx International, Inc.
1725 Clearwater-Largo Road S.
Post Office Box 25
Clearwater, Fl 34617
Tel. (813) 587-0999

Note: The law changes constantly and is subject to different interpretations. It is up to you to check it thoroughly before relying on it. Neither the author nor the publisher guarantees the outcome of the uses to which this material is put.

First Edition, September, 1992

ISBN 0-913825-51-4
Library of Congress Catalog Number: 91-067129

Manufactured in the United States of America.

This publication is designed to provide accurate and authoritative information in regard to the subject matter covered. It is sold with the understanding that the publisher is not engaged in rendering legal, accounting or other professional services. If legal advice or other expert assistance is required, the service of a competent professional person should be sought.

> - From a Declaration of Principles jointly adopted by a Committee of the American Bar Association and a Committee of Publishers.

Published by Sphinx Publishing, a division of Sphinx International, Inc., Post Office Box 25, Clearwater, Florida 34617. For pricing in the United States call 800-226-5291, overseas and Canada call 813-587-0999.

TABLE OF CONTENTS

i

DEDICATION

To the memory of my beloved father, Ramon, and of my mother, Leonor, who were the first and most important "immigrants" in my life. They not only had the vision of a new life in the United States but also the courage to implement that vision. In the spirit of my parents' dreams and motivations, this book is also dedicated to all of you who aspire to participate in the American dream.

FOREWORD

It is a rank understatement to say that much has changed in the world since the first edition of this book was published in 1989. Yet, there is no better way of putting this work into perspective than to recount some of those changes, since directly or indirectly they affect the purpose and scope of this book.

First and foremost, insofar as concerns this book, there was enacted the Immigration and Naturalization Act of 1990. This act, known in this book as IMMACT90, implemented some fundamental changes in the immigration system and it will probably continue to be the substantive law in this field for the foreseeable future - granted, that in light of current world events, the term "foreseeable future" is itself a term of art. This book will try to explain the changes inherent in the IMMACT90 in a manner that will be understandable to the lay public, especially to the foreign person, whatever his/her occupation and or station in life may be. The book will discuss those features of the law that are likely to apply to most persons seeking entry to the United States. It will not attempt to be the definitive scholarly or technical work in this area, for even as we write, administrative rules and regulations are being drafted that will implement and interpret the law.

The rest of the world also has changed. The "Cold War" between the Communist East and the Capitalist West is over, or at least, has changed dramatically. Germany has been united. The former Warsaw Pact countries have abandoned the traditional Marxist/Leninist school of communism and have adopted or are trying to adopt more traditional market based economies and concomitantly have adopted political institutions which more closely resemble Western style democracies.

The Union of Soviet Socialist Republics no longer exists. The era of Gorbachev has come and gone in a whirlwind of events that has staggered the sensitivities of even the most eclectic of political analysts. In place of the former U.S.S.R. there has emerged the Commonwealth of Independent States which will probably never have the central authority of its predecessor state. We now speak of Georgians, Ukranians, Russians and have dropped the word "soviets" from our language.

In the first few months of 1991, the United States under the authority of the United Nations carried out an intense and technologically awesome military campaign against the country of Iraq which resulted in the "liberation" of Kuwait and the re-establishment of the primacy of United States military prowess on a world scale.

At the same time that it has demonstrated its military abilities, the United States has experienced an economic recession which has revealed some inherent weaknesses and limitations of the U.S. economic system, all of which nontheless confirm the ultimate strength and resilience of that economy. Compared to the almost total collapse of the economy of the former U.S.S.R., the ability of the United States to survive the present economic stagnation confirms its economy's fundamental strengths. Japan has emerged as a true world "super power" with the ability to influence world economic events and conditions without the necessity of projecting any significant military capability whatsoever.

Perhaps all these events manifest the unfolding of a new era in which the old and overused aphorism "it's a small world" will have a more poignant and relevant meaning to all of us.

INTRODUCTION

I am sure the reader has heard the expression, "The gift of youth is wasted on the young." The premise of this book is that the knowledge of the law is often wasted on the lawyers. We lawyers frequently complain that if our clients had done (or not done) this, that or the other we could have done a better job resolving their legal problems. Of course, the reason our clients didn't do what they should have done was because they didn't know what the law required in the first place. The knowledge that the client needed was not available to him at the time he was making his decision. So, in the normal course of events the client takes presumably responsible action and then seeks out the lawyer for advice or reinforcement after the fact. Since the client has already pursued a given course of action, the legal consultant, frequently, can only comment on the appropriateness of the client's action. This, of course, is an unfortunate legal irony because lay people, even knowledgeable business people, are not always familiar with technical legal requirements applicable to a specific situation in the United States.

In the complex field of immigration and visa law (we'll call it "visa law" in this book) an early mistake can frustrate or, at the least, complicate a person's plan to move himself and/or his business to the United States. We will try in this book to address this situation by explaining in practical terms the philosophy and logic in the United States immigration regimen.

This book was conceived as a collection of useful information which I have over the years customarily conveyed to foreign persons during my initial office interviews with them. It was apparent to me that most foreign persons (aliens), regardless of their country of origin, were asking the same general type of questions. The client wanted to understand the system in order to understand why (s)he was required to reveal and submit certain types of information. In order to provide a thoroughly useful service to the client, I had to explain to the client much of the background of the law, as well as the philosophy and "mind set" of the U.S. immigration and consular authorities. From my perspective, by thoroughly informing the client, I am able to obtain from the client the type of information which enables me to give the best advice in the planning of his/her entry into the United States. As I began to write a compendium of educational articles and memoranda, it grew into this book which I hope will provide the reader with some of the insights which this writer feels are essential in successfully fulfilling his/her immigration motivations, both long and short term. The book also assist the client to learn quickly some of the most important and immediate business and legal norms and customs that he would encounter in the United States.

As of the writing of this updated version of this book, the United States had just enacted the **Immigration Act of 1990** (IMMACT90). This act implements the most substantial and broad revisions of the United States immigration regimen in the last forty (40) years. It will probably define the immigration policy of the United States for the immediate future, subject, of course, to gradual technical refinement and judicial interpretation. This book will cover the major provisions of this law as they would apply to a foreign person who is contemplating a move to the United States, whether that move be permanent or temporary. The book will not cover many technical provisions of the law which apply to a person already within the United States. As further described in this Introduction, the purpose of the book is to educate the foreign person with respect to the policy and philosophy of the United States Immigration regimen and not to encourage a lay person to handle or manage any particular immigration process on his own. Indeed, the very complex nature of this process militates against the "self help" approach and consultation with a trained professional legal consultant is greatly encouraged.

There are certain countries in the world where there is an especially heavy demand for immigrant visas to the U.S. or where there is a history of fraud and abuse with respect to visa application to the United States. The United States consular authorities in those countries are very scrupulous in examining an individual's credentials and intentions when the individual applies for any kind of visa to the United States. This book should be especially helpful to persons from those countries, however, it will also be helpful to <u>any</u> non-U.S. person seeking to enter the U.S. since it is easy to overlook the strict standards applied by the United States immigration authorities to <u>all</u> persons entering the U.S.

This publication is especially directed at business persons and investors to whom immigration concerns may be secondary to other strategic business planning. It will also be useful for other persons, whether they be students or immediate relatives of U.S. citizens or permanent resident aliens. It is not the author's purpose to encourage nor discourage immigration or the transfer of capital to the United States. Rather, the book is offered in the context of certain political, economic, and sociological factors over which the author has no control or ability to affect. These factors can be summarized as follows:

1. <u>The relative ease of international transportation and communication.</u> This phenomenon has created the illusion that political and national boundaries are of less importance now than in the past. The mass media as a result of technological advances during the past few decades has projected the United States culture and way of life to the most remote parts of the world. Thus, many persons in foreign countries may be quite familiar with certain of the more attractive cultural characteristics of the United States. This may lead a person to feel that he already shares "a part of" the United States lifestyle.

2. <u>The interdependence of national economies.</u> As a result of some of the technological advances already mentioned, the community of nations' business and commerce is more interrelated and interdependent. This often requires the transfer of business personnel to the United States. This, of course, is often a bilateral process with many expansive U.S. firms transferring their U.S. employees to other parts of the world as well. The world economy often pays little heed to national boundaries and companies and individuals are often substantially affected by the events or prognostications of financial centers far removed from their home offices.

There is a growing body of opinion which hypothesizes that there is only one actual **world** economy and financial market, with three (3) regional centers, ie., Tokyo, New York and London; and that these centers are so interrelated that the cause and effect sequence as to their individual influence on the world economy is academic since each center is so closely dependent upon and influential of the others that their combined effects on the world's economy is a constant force.

3. <u>The relative strength and adaptability of the U.S. economy.</u> This reality makes the United States an attractive market for foreign investment, both on a large and a small scale. The entrepreneurial spirit reacts much the same way to this fact, whether it be that of a large multinational firm or of a smaller business whose owners are very often also its key employees. This fact coupled with the recent weakening of the U. S. Dollar makes business acquisitions in the United States very attractive--especially real estate.

4. <u>The United States is a politically stable country.</u> In addition to being politically stable the United States has a history of <u>relative</u> tolerance for immigrants from foreign countries--especially for those immigrants who share an affinity for the capitalist ideology. There are pockets of ethnic communities throughout the U.S. where a foreign person of a particular ethnic background can feel ethnically secure and find the familiar cultural characteristics of his home country. The United States is a geographically diverse country

with regions resembling those of other countries. Furthermore, various geographic areas of the United States offer pleasant climate conditions as well as attractive and modern urban, suburban and agricultural areas. There is someplace for everyone.

As a result of the above factors, there is a tremendous worldwide demand for both permanent and temporary visas to the United States. This has caused the United States immigration authorities to control the quality, quantity and character of inward migration. However, the collision of these two drives causes many human and business problems, many of which can be avoided or minimized through proper planning.

This, then, is the setting for the writing of this book. The author's intention is to teach the major visa considerations that a prospective immigrant or temporary visitor must understand in order to logically and intelligently plan an entry into the United States. This work may be criticized by certain members of the immigration legal community as being too simplistic and for not providing enough detail on certain intricacies involved in the administrative and legal processes involved in the procurement of visas for foreign persons. We accept such anticipated criticism by stating that we do not intend this book to replace the services of competent professional guidance. Indeed, the book recognizes that professional assistance, not just in the field of law, but also in the disciplines of accounting, marketing, finance, etc., is very often critical in making successful long-term decisions respecting business/visa matters.

The purpose of the book is to prepare and educate the individual (and/or his employees) so he and/or his professional consultant may comply with the requirements of the United States immigration regimen. It is our purpose to teach the methodology and bureaucratic psychology of the U.S. Immigration regimen, since an understanding of these principles will enable a person or company to adapt to the overall situation as otherwise applies to him.

As to those who would criticize us for including more detail than the average person is willing to learn, our response is, in all respect, that this book is not written for the average person. It is written for that special person who in search of economic and personal improvement desires to expand his life activities and those of his business beyond the borders of his home country, by transferring some or all of those activities into the most dynamic society on this planet, the United States of America.

SECTION I

THE VISA SYSTEM IN GENERAL

Every time a foreign person comes to the border of the United States seeking entry, even if only for a normal holiday visit, he confronts the formidable immigration regimen of the United States. The term "Immigration" in the context of this book includes every significant physical entry into the territory of the United States, whether the purpose of the entry be for a temporary visit with a specific end time or for a permanent relocation.

The immigration system of the United States is the product of various unique historical and political forces which produce some seemingly incongruous policies. On the one hand the system can seem very liberal and generous with respect to its procedural processes and yet extremely restrictive about its substantive admission policies. It is a system of seeming contradictions which must be understood in its historical and political context.

1.1 - BRIEF LEGAL/HISTORICAL CONTEXT. The United States was founded by immigrants, that is, by people who were not originally from the nation. Yet, the Constitution of the United States, the organic document which established the unique political existence of this nation, is almost silent on the entire question of immigration. There is only a fleeting mention of this subject in that document and it does not contain a political or philosophical articulation of a policy or system of immigration. The U. S. Congress is simply authorized to make the laws concerning immigration.

History tells us that during the first one hundred fifty (150) years, the motivating force for immigration to the United States was privation and persecution abroad. People came to the United States to escape negative forces in their home countries. They came to this country fully expecting to experience personal sacrifice in exchange for political, economic and/or religious freedom. From the late 19th century onward people immigrated to the United States for economic and human survival. Immigration came in waves of specific nationalities and numbers to escape conditions such as drought, famine, depression, religious persecution, etc. in their countries of origin. That is still the case today.

Until the end of the 19th Century there was basically no control or limitation on immigration to the United States. Starting from 1882, however a series of general immigration statutes were enacted which were principally a reaction to the type and numbers of people who had previously entered. From that year forward, the United States embarked on a series of restrictions on immigration. Thus, specific national origins quotas were imposed from time to time which were ethnically and/or racially discriminatory. Quantitative restrictions were introduced into the immigration regimen in 1921 with the passage of the first quota system applicable to designated nationalities.

With the passage of the McCARRAN-WALTER ACT in 1952, which law formed the basic structure of the Immigration Law as we know it today, a new phenomenon began to emerge. The U.S. immigration system began to partake of a more democratic character and the law attempted to apply admissions policies without direct regard to national and or racial origins. The last trace of racial or ethnic discrimination was removed with the abolition of the separate quota for Western Hemisphere aliens in 1978.

As a result of the passage of the Immigration Act of 1990, the immigration regimen with respect to permanent visas now emphasizes the policy of attracting persons who possess desirable occupational skills or economic resources. The law still provides for the unification of families and close relatives of U.S. citizens and, to a lesser extent, of permanent residents. The law now for the first time establishes a category for the issuance of permanent visas to investors who establish or invest in new, job creating enterprises. There have also been some substantial changes with respect to the issuance of temporary visas to the United States. One reality is constant and indisputable: There is a higher demand for visas, permanent and temporary, to the United States than there is supply and/or perceived need therefor. With this general background, let us look more closely at the United States visa system.

The United States <u>federal</u> government has jurisdiction over all visa and immigration matters. The individual State and local governments have only a limited role in this field, such as the initial processing of labor certification applications. As an illustration of this point, I would point out that the quality and strength of the alien's connection with State and local governmental and business institutions are of very limited help in qualifying for a long-term visa. This elementary fact is very often overlooked by foreign persons who do not understand the nature of the federal system of government in the United States. In fact, the programs and policies of a State about a particular subject can be diametrically different from those of the federal government on the same subject. Unfortunately, if the subject matter in question is one which the <u>Constitution of the United States</u> assigns to the federal government then the federal law takes precedence over the state law. This is the reality with matters concerning United States immigration policy.

Failure to fulfill all of the detailed requirements of the United States visa system can often result in a denial or delay in the issuance of a visa petition even if the local or state authorities welcome the person and/or his investment. In short, neither the Immigration and Naturalization Service nor the U.S. Consul abroad depends upon the recommendations of the local or state Chambers of Commerce, community service organizations, etc. The alien entering the United States must comply with the formal requirements of a Federal bureaucratic system that is largely insulated from "outside" interests.

<u>1.2 - U.S. CONSULATES ABROAD.</u> Outside of the United States the alien deals almost exclusively with the United States Consulate or Embassy in his home country. The United States Consul has, within the confines of the law, almost complete discretion as to whom and under what circumstances a visa to the United States will be granted. Furthermore, there is no appeal from a denial of a visa by the U.S. consul other than for interpretations of law. In practical terms this means that an alien should have a thorough understanding of the law, and should be thoroughly prepared and documented to comply with the law **before** the alien first approaches the U.S. consul on any visa question. Please read the previous sentence again and accept it as a fundamental principal in dealing with the host country United States consulate with respect to visa matters.

In addition, the local U.S. Consul abroad probably has an in depth understanding of political and economic conditions of that country and is able to apply that knowledge and experience to individual petitions of companies and persons who are residents of the host country.

<u>1.3 - THE IMMIGRATION AND NATURALIZATION SERVICE.</u> If the alien is already in the United States, then he must deal with the Immigration and Naturalization Service (INS). This agency is a division of the Office of the United States Attorney General and operates through various regional and subregional offices throughout the United States. A list of these offices is found in the Appendix A of this book.

Once an alien is in the United States, he has more procedural rights than would be the case if he were outside the United States.

Certain visa petitions such as the I-129 (used for the L-1 visa) must be filed within the United States at a regional office of the Immigration & Naturalization Service. Other visa petitions such as for the B-1 visa are filed abroad at the U.S. Consulate. As of the writing of this book there were four (4) Regional Service Centers and there are discussions underway to consolidate the operations of two or more of these for purposes of efficiency and consistency. Indeed, the business visa petitions have already been routed from the Southern Regional Service Center in Irving, Texas to the Eastern Regional Service Center in St. Albans, Vermont. The regional service centers are essentially "think tanks", access to which from the public, including even immigration attorneys, is severely limited. The philosophy is to ensure that visa petitions will be adjudicated in an objective manner. The result has sometimes been that adjudications are sometimes accomplished in a hypertechnical manner with little regard for the realities of life and business.

Regardless of how a foreign person may have entered the United States, after his entry he is under the jurisdiction of the INS.

1.4 - INSPECTION, EXCLUSION AND DEPORTATION.

The United States has, as does every other nation in the world, complete discretion as to whom it will admit within its borders. When an alien appears at the border or other port of entry, he is subject to the power of <u>inspection</u> and <u>exclusion</u> by the Immigration inspector. The purpose of the inspection is to determine whether or not the foreign person is admissible to the United States. The inspecting officer will examine the passport and visa to assure himself that the physical person in front of him is the person identified in the travel documents. Additionally, the officer will, by interrogation and/or physical inspection of luggage and/or of the person, determine whether the person is entitled to enter the United States in the visa category requested and for how long that duration should be granted. Lately, the duration of stay under particular visa categories has been established by regulation, so that in most instances the immigration inspector is bound by the term established in the applicable regulation or operating instruction. Normally, the actual inspection time takes only a few minutes unless the inspecting officer suspects an irregularity.

Upon inspection and in accordance with law, the U. S. Immigration officer may <u>exclude</u> an alien from entering the United States, if he finds the alien ineligible to enter the U.S. This power to exclude is the primary obstacle to an alien entering the United States. It should be noted that many foreign persons complain of rudeness on the part of the INS inspectors at the ports of entry. This writer has, in fact, witnessed unnecessary rudeness and meanness on the part of some inspectors and other INS officers and has also witnessed courtesy and civility on the part of other INS officers. The INS inspector often views himself as a police official trying to prevent illegal entry into the United States rather than as a good will emissary of the United States. This unfortunate attitude is reinforced by the strong demands for visas to the United States and by continuous attempts by certain aliens to circumvent the law and attempt to enter the United States illegally. I can only warn the alien reader of this fact, so that he/she will not be overly intimidated by the sometimes jaundiced reception he/she may receive at the point of entry. If the foreign person reads this book and understands how the immigration system functions, he/she will get through the border with the least amount of upset and inconvenience.

A decision by the IMMIGRATION & NATURALIZATION SERVICE officer to exclude a person from entry into the United States is difficult to reverse on appeal. Even a person with a valid visa may be excluded or admitted provisionally on parole or under a process called "deferred inspection" at the border if the immigration official determines or suspects that the alien is not entitled to use the visa in his passport.

1.5 - GENERAL GROUNDS FOR EXCLUSION. IMMACT90 enacted broad and profound changes with respect to the grounds for the exclusion of aliens to the United States. For the most part, the changes wrought by IMMACT90 represent an improvement over the archaic concepts of exclusion that existed under the prior law. The alien encounters the concept of exclusion when he/she appears at the U.S. Consulate and applies for a visa and, again, when he/she appears at the border and attempts to enter the United States. Thus, an alien might have the visa petition denied by the U.S. consular office because the consular office believes that one or more grounds of excludability may apply to the particular alien. The consular officer's decision is very difficult to reverse since he/she is granted broad discretionary latitude in interpreting the factual circumstances surrounding any particular alien petitioner. Even if the alien already has a proper visa in his possession, the Immigration and Naturalization inspector at the border may deny the alien entry to the United States on the basis that one or more of the following grounds for exclusion might apply to the foreign person. With respect to certain of the grounds for exclusion, the law provides "waivers" or exemptions which may, nonetheless, permit a foreign person to enter the United States even though one or more grounds for exclusion may apply. When the term "waiver" is used in the context of exclusion, it refers to an exception or a pardon of the offending conduct. In essence, a waiver is a form of a pardon as to the offending conduct.

(1). HEALTH-RELATED GROUNDS: The first grounds for exclusion are what are known as health-related grounds. These would apply to any foreign person who is found by the Department of Health and Human Services to have a communicable disease of public health significance. This would include, for instance, any person who has been diagnosed as being HIV positive. This category of exclusion would also apply to any other form of communicable disease such as Tuberculosis.

This exclusion would apply to any foreign person determined by the Department of Health and Human Services to have a physical or mental disorder or to manifest any behavior that could or that has in the past posed a threat to others. The determination that a particular person has a physical or mental disorder will be made on a case by case basis because this is essentially a new provision. How the method and scope of enforcement of the new law will differ from the prior law is not clear.

If the Department of Health and Human Services finds that the alien is a drug abuser or a drug addict, the alien could be excluded from entry. This exclusion provision is separate from the criminal provision which would bar any person from entering the United States who has been convicted of any criminal offense involving drug use. Apparently experimentation alone will not render a foreign person excludable, but it is not clear what conduct would be included in the exception of mere "experimentation". IMMACT90 also provides grounds for discretionary relief against exclusion if the foreign person has necessary family ties and otherwise proves mitigating circumstances which would move the Immigration and Naturalization Service to waive this ground of exclusion and permit the alien to enter the United States in spite of being found to be a drug abuser or addict. The purpose for the waiver provision is to keep families together and to prevent a hardship where a proper family environment would mitigate any danger to the public. The law also provides that grounds for exclusion on this basis may be waived if a bond is provided.

(2). CRIMINAL GROUNDS: There are essentially five grounds for exclusion on the basis of criminal conduct:

A.   Conviction or admission of a crime of moral turpitude or a crime involving a drug offense. An exception to this category of exclusion would be minor offenses, which is defined as offenses for which the sentence imposed is less than six months. It is important to understand the concept of crimes of "moral turpitude". This designation refers to those crimes that are indicative of bad moral character, such as crimes of theft, assault and battery, murder, rape and the like. There is an exception to this exclusion if the crime was committed by an alien who was under the age of 18 at the time of the commission of the crime; and the crime was committed more than five years before the date of application for the visa. Another exception to excludability applies to crimes for which the maximum possible penalty does not exceed one year and, if the alien was actually convicted of the crime, where the alien was not in fact sentenced to a term of imprisonment in excess of six months.

B.   Conviction of two or more crimes if the combined custodial sentence imposed is for five years or longer regardless of whether or not the crime arose from a single stream of events or whether or not the crimes were of moral turpitude.

C.   When the consular or immigration officer knows or has reason to believe that the alien is or was a drug trafficker or was a person who aided or abetted or conspired in drug trafficking.

D.   Any alien who was involved in prostitution or is coming to the United States to engage in any other unlawful commercialized vice.

E.   Aliens involved in serious criminal activity who have asserted immunity from prosecution and departed. This would apply, for instance, to persons who committed crimes or committed acts which could have been crimes, but who asserted diplomatic immunity. Waivers of excludability on the above grounds may be available under section 212H of IMMACT90 for non-drug-related crimes, for prostitution or for conviction of a single offense of possession of 30 grams or less of marijuana. The waiver is available upon either the passage of 15 years from the disqualifying event or in the event of extreme hardship to designated U.S. citizen or permanent resident relatives, ie., spouse, parent, son, or daughter.

(3). SECURITY AND RELATED GROUNDS: This category of exclusion would apply to:

A.   Any person who, in the opinion of the U.S. Consular Officer, entered the United States to engage in prejudicial and unlawful activities which would include espionage, sabotage, and violation or evasion of laws concerning the prohibition of export from the United States of goods, technology or other sensitive information. There is a waiver possible for anyone who violates the provision concerning the export of technology, if the person seeks to re-enter the United States solely as a nonimmigrant.

B.   Anyone who is engaged in terrorist activity or who is an active member of the PLO. Terrorist activity is defined to encompass active support for terrorist organizations through a variety of activities, including fund-raising. Terrorist activity in this case is defined to apply immediately to an person who is an officer, official, representative or spokesman of the Palestinian Liberation Organization. This is one questionably discriminatory section of the statute which I believe will be subject to judicial scrutiny. Terrorist activity also includes, of course, high-jacking or sabotage of any conveyance which includes aircraft or vessels; killing, detaining or threatening to kill or injure another individual in order to compel a third person in order to do or abstain from doing any act as an explicit condition for the release of the individual, as well as a violent attack upon an internationally protected person. Anyone who is involved in assassination to engage in terrorist activity also is defined to include "an act which the actor knows or reasonably should know affords material support to any individual, organization or government in conducting a terrorist activity at any time, including any of the following acts:

Providing any type of material support, including a safehouse, transportation, communications, funds, false identification, weapons, explosives, training through any individual the actor knows or has reason to believe has committed or plans to commit an act of terrorist activity, or anyone who solicits funds or other things of value for terrorist activities or terrorist organizations.

C.	Anyone whose entry would have a foreign policy consequence seriously adverse to the interests of the United States. This is a general exclusionary right given the U.S. Consulate. Exceptions to exclusion on these grounds are made for foreign government officials and politicians in cases in which their exclusion would be based upon speech or association which would have been lawful in the U.S.

D.	Other individuals who are not foreign government officials who intend to engage in speech or association which also would be lawful in the U.S., but this is also subject to veto by personal determination of Secretary of State based upon a compelling U.S. foreign policy interest.

E.	Also excludable would be an alien who seeks to apply for immigrant status and who was a member or is actively a member in a communist or totalitarian party. An exception to excludability on this basis is available for those persons who were members of the Communist party on an involuntary basis or who were members when they were under the age of 16. An additional exception to excludability is available to persons whose membership terminated two years before the visa application was made. If the totalitarian party still controls the alien's country, then an exception can be made for a former Communist party member only if his/her membership terminated at least five years previous to application for entry.

Waivers or exceptions to these grounds of excludability are available for any of the above aliens who are close and dependent family relatives of U.S. citizens if they are otherwise not a threat to U.S. security.

F.	Anyone who participated in the NAZI persecution of World War II or in genocide. There is an exception to this exclusionary ground for those persons who are seeking to enter the United States only as diplomatic representatives.

(4) PERSONS LIKELY TO BECOME A PUBLIC CHARGE: This category of excludability applies to persons who are or are likely to become a public charge. This means an inability to support themselves. This grounds may be avoided by an undertaking or affidavit of a U.S. citizen guaranteeing that the alien will not need to be supported by the public.

(5) PROTECTION OF THE U.S. LABOR MARKET: This category of exclusion applies to persons who are entering the United States seeking to engage in gainful employment. Anyone who seeks to enter the United States to work and who does not have a Labor Certification from the United States Department of Labor is excludable. In this regard, please see section 2.8 of this book on page 20 for job-related visa preferences.

(6) PHYSICIANS: Also excludable under this designation would be those physicians who are unqualified to practice medicine in the United States. In order for a physician to enter the United States, he or she must have passed an English proficiency test and must have taken one of two national medical exams.

(7) ILLEGAL ENTRY INTO THE UNITED STATES: This category includes:

A.   Persons who have previously entered the United States illegally and who are otherwise violators of the United States immigration law. Anyone who has already been excluded from entry to the United States is barred from re-entry into the United States for one year.

B.   Any alien who has been previously deported from the United States. Such a person is barred from re-entry into the United States for five years, but in the case of someone who has been deported as an aggravated felon, the exclusion applies for a period of 20 years. An aggravated felon includes all persons charged with drug trafficking offenses.

C.   Persons guilty of material misrepresentation with respect to any petition or other document with respect to a visa. This provision bars foreign persons from entering the United States who seek or have sought to obtain a visa, documentation, entry or other immigration benefit by committing fraud or otherwise willfully misrepresenting material facts. There is a waiver for this exclusion ground for those persons who are immediate relatives of U.S. citizens or of permanent resident aliens or for cases where the fraud occurred at least ten years before entry. These grounds of waiver of excludability apply only to persons seeking to enter the United States as immigrants.

D.   Stowaways and Smugglers of aliens. Waivers of excludability are available to aliens guilty of smuggling their immediate family members. This section, however, would not apply to anyone engaged in the smuggling of a person into the United States for profit.

E.   Document Fraud. Any alien who has been found in a proceeding to have used, provided or attempted to provide false documentation.

(8)   **ENTERING WITHOUT PROPER DOCUMENTS:** These grounds of excludability apply to aliens who do not have a valid visa or entry document or who do not have the required documents in support of their immigration status upon entry.

There are general waiver provisions applicable to the above grounds for exclusion.

(9)   **PERSONS INELIGIBLE FOR CITIZENSHIP:** This category of exclusion applies to persons who are ineligible for citizenship because of violating military service requirements and who are draft evaders.

(10)   **PERSONS WHO INTEND TO PRACTICE POLYGAMY**

(11)   **ALIEN GUARDIANS ACCOMPANYING EXCLUDED ALIENS**

(12)   **INTERNATIONAL CHILD ABDUCTORS.** This ground applies to an alien who may be involved in a domestic (family) dispute involving child custody. During these rather emotional controversies, an alien may be tempted to simply remove him/herself and the couple's children from the United States and bring them to his/her country of origin and thus thwart the possibility of the U.S. citizen acquiring child custody rights. Under U.S. and international law, such conduct is improper and amounts to domestic abduction. An alien who is found to be an international child abductor is excludable without relief. There are no waivers available for such a person.

If any of the above categories of exclusion apply, the alien who is considering making a visa application to the United States should consult a qualified U.S. immigration attorney before submitting the application. The above categories can also be grounds for deportation in the event the alien enters the country by misrepresentation or omission of information.

"Deportation" is the term for the removal of aliens who have already entered the United States. In deportation proceedings, there is available a wider array of appellate procedures and safeguards since the law presumes that the alien is here under the color of law, and his rights are, therefore, protected under the U.S. Constitution. The grounds for deportation from the United States as well as the defenses and waivers applicable to deportation are beyond the scope of this book.

1.6 - DISTINCTION BETWEEN IMMIGRANT AND NON-IMMIGRANT VISAS. There are generally two types of visas available to foreign persons seeking to enter the United States. The first is a permanent visa (also known colloquially as a "green card"), and the other is a non-permanent visa, or temporary visa. There is only one type of permanent visa, and once that is obtained, there are no special subclassifications or conditions attached to that visa -- except as to the two (2) year condition placed on employment creation visas, discussed further on in this book. So that regardless of how a person obtained a green card, whether as a result of marriage to a U.S. citizen or as a result of a labor certification or by other family relationship to a U.S. citizen, the resulting visa consequences are the same in every case. The permanent visa enables that person to live and work where ever he chooses without distinction as to how the visa was obtained. There are, however, many different types of temporary visas, and each visa has its own set of qualifications and conditions, both as to its duration and as to the activities the alien may lawfully undertake in the United States in accordance with the visa. **Section I** of this book will discuss the permanent visas and **Section II** will discuss some of the most important temporary visas for most people. Which category of visa, i.e., permanent or temporary, is the most appropriate for a foreign person depends upon many factors deserving of study and consideration, not the least of which is the alien's own intention.

1.7 - THE PROBLEM OF INTENT. An important piece of information to be learned from this book and probably the most important concept to be understood by any foreign person is the importance attached by the immigration authorities to the alien's intention as to duration of stay and purpose in the U.S. An example: A **permanent** visa is given only to a qualified person who intends to remain living in the United States permanently, while a **temporary** (non-immigrant) visa is issued only to a qualified person who intends to stay in the United States for a temporary period and then depart. In the latter case, if the alien's immediate intention is to remain permanently in the United States, then the only type of visa for which he can qualify is the immigrant visa. Looking at it in reverse, the alien would <u>not</u> be qualified for a temporary visa if he has an immediate intention to remain in the United States permanently, even though he might be otherwise qualified to obtain that temporary visa.

There are exceptions to this rule, but in general, an alien who meets the objective qualifications for a non-immigrant visa will be denied that visa or entry to the United States under that visa if the U.S. Consul abroad or the INS examining officer at the border feels that the alien's true intention is to remain in the U.S. permanently. Furthermore, every alien entering the United States is presumed to be an immigrant (and thus excludable) unless he can demonstrate that he has a valid non-immigrant visa in his possession and is entitled to enter the United States under that visa.

In the event the immigration border inspector determines that a foreign person is not entitled to enter the United States, he can deny to that foreign person the right to enter and require that person to return to his country of origin. In most cases, however, the officer will permit the foreign person to enter the United States on "parole" and then schedule a formal hearing at the local office of the Immigration and Naturalization Service to determine whether or not the person should be "excluded" or permitted to remain in the United States.

Thus, instead of a "welcome", there is a "keep out" attitude framed in the law. This has two possible practical consequences. First, the U.S. Consul in the foreign country will only grant a non-immigrant visa if he is satisfied that the person will return to his home country. If the U.S. Consul is not so convinced, then he may deny issuance of the visa, regardless of whether the alien meets the other objective qualifications for the issuance of the visa. Secondly, the alien may be "excluded" at the border if the immigration officer is convinced that the person's intent on entering the U.S. is different from that required by the visa in his passport, or is otherwise not entitled to enter the United States. The above four (4) paragraphs should be re-read and thoroughly understood.

An example of the first situation can be illustrated by the problem many Iranians encountered after the Iranian revolution when they tried to obtain visas to the United States as visitors (tourists). Even though many of the applicants were well-respected business people with homes and property in Iran, experience taught the U.S. consuls that most people leaving Iran would never return, regardless of the cost to them of their abandoned property. The same problem exists for persons coming from other troubled spots in the world. Thus, the question of intention is absolutely critical in many cases and is subject to the almost unfettered discretion of the U.S. consul abroad. This statement is not meant to be a criticism of the State Department practice; it merely reflects reality.

This is a true story which illustrates this problem. A young Lebanese man who was married to a U.S. citizen and was himself a permanent resident alien wanted to bring his parents who were Lebanese citizens to visit with him in the United States. He sought my assistance because his parents' application for visitors' visas (B-2) had been denied by various U.S. consuls in Europe. His parents had left Lebanon and were in Europe trying to obtain U.S. visitors' visas. I explained that B-2 visas are issued abroad and that there was little that I could do for them here in the United States other than to suggest some documentation that they should present to the U.S. Consul. Nonetheless I telephoned various U.S. Consuls in Europe to see if I could help. I was told by all of them that based upon their experience most business people leaving Lebanon were doing so with the intention of never returning.

I suggested to the young man that he might offer to provide a cash bond guaranteeing to the U.S. Consul where his parents were located that his parents would depart the U.S. at the conclusion of their visit. After speaking with the U.S. consul in a particular European country, I suggested that the young man travel to that U.S. consul and plead his case directly. The young man noted all that I told him and left. Some months later while I was shopping in a local department store this same young fellow approached me and identified himself to me as the person in this story. I asked him about his parents. He told me that he had traveled to the U.S. consular post in Europe, had convinced the consul his parents would return to Lebanon after their visit, and that his parents then obtained their visitors' visas. I congratulated him on his fine efforts and asked him how his parents enjoyed their visit to the United States. He then told me that his parents, after spending some time in the United States, decided that they were not returning to their home country. Since he had recently become a U.S. citizen he was filing an immediate relative petition to obtain their permanent residency for them. This was precisely what the U.S. Consul with whom I had spoken on the telephone predicted would happen.

As stated previously, obtaining a non-immigrant visa abroad is no guarantee that the alien will be admitted to the United States. An example of this is the story of the European young person with a valid non-immigrant visa who was turned away at the border because of his idle and nervous chatter with the immigration officer. The person emphasized his happiness at finally being in the United States, and his unwillingness to ever return to his cold and inhospitable country again. Whether or not the story's details have been exaggerated is not important. The important point to note is that upon arrival at the border a foreign person must prove that his intent coincides with the visa in his passport.

The question of intent arises when a person who has a permanent visa leaves the United States for an extended period of time. The law presumes that if a permanent resident alien leaves the United States for one year or more, this absence from the U.S. can be considered an abandonment of his visa. Permanent resident aliens contemplating a long but temporary stay outside the United States should, therefore, make that fact known to the immigration authorities before departure to obtain a re-entry permit that will permit return to the United States even after the extended absence. The permanent resident will be able to retain the permanent residency visa if the reason for the extended stay abroad is for valid reasons beyond his/her control

The question of intent also arises within the context of different types of NON-IMMIGRANT visas. For example, if a person enters the United States as a tourist with a B-2 visa and then shortly after his entry applies for a change to a different type of visa the Immigration and Naturalization authorities will require an explanation as to why the individual did not originally apply in his home country for the visa which he now seeks by way of change. If the Immigration and Naturalization Service officials do not receive a satisfactory explanation they may deny the change of status based upon a form of fraud known as "preconceived intent". The Immigration and Naturalization Service will infer that the alien gained entry to the United States by way of the tourist visa with a preconceived intent of applying for a different visa status shortly after arrival.

We will treat the question of intention throughout this book, and we will discuss its consequences in various circumstances. Thus, the foreign person must accept that his intention will be under scrutiny by the U.S. immigration and consular authorities when he/she applies for any type of visa.

1.8 UNAUTHORIZED EMPLOYMENT. In 1986, the United States took direct action concerning the problem of enforcing its laws against unauthorized employment by aliens in the United States. It sought to accomplish this goal by imposing civil and criminal penalties on U.S. employers who employ aliens who are not legally authorized to work. This law renders it difficult for aliens who are not authorized to work to engage in meaningful employment, since it exposes their employers to legal sanctions. The employer, thus, becomes part of the enforcement apparatus as a result of its self interest in avoiding the civil and criminal sanctions imposed by the law. The employer is required to file a form (I-9) which establishes the documentation that the alien presented to the employer to verify the alien's authorization to work. Of course, in addition to the employer sanctions, the alien is also still subject to deportation if he/she is found to be engaged in unauthorized employment.

The law provides for the grant of work authorization to certain aliens who are in the United States and who might not otherwise be eligible to work. Thus, aliens for whom an immigrant visa is immediately available, such as immediate relatives of U.S. citizens may obtain work authorization. In addition, aliens who are being processed for asylum claims or who are otherwise in deportation proceedings may on a discretionary basis be issued work authorization. In most cases, an identity card, know as an EAD (Employment Authorization Document), with a photograph of the alien, is issued as documentation of this coveted status. Attached to this book as an Exhibit is the instruction sheet for the Form I-765, which is very helpful in defining the bases for the issuance of work authorization.

SECTION II

PERMANENT IMMIGRANT VISA

The United States establishes two general categories of persons who may immigrate permanently to the United States, i.e., persons who are subject to an annual worldwide numerical limit and those persons who may immigrate at any time regardless of the worldwide demand for immigrant visas. The first group of persons is subject to a system of categories or "preferences" which determines the priority of admission based on the applicable annual quota. For fiscal year 1992, which starts on October 1, 1991, through fiscal year 1994 the annual quota is 700,000 persons. For fiscal years 1995 and thereafter the annual quota is 675,000 persons. This is the **preference system** for permanent visas.

There is a second group of persons who are not subject to the **preference system** and who, when qualified, may enter the United States regardless of the numerical quota system. These are known as "non-preference" immigrants. This category includes refugees (who have their own quota), persons provided permanent residency under special provisions of law for agricultural workers ("SAW", "RAW" programs), immediate relatives of U.S. citizens, and children born to a permanent resident during a temporary visit outside the United States. Most persons entering the U.S. as non-preference immigrants are related in a determined degree to U.S. citizens. In this book we will distinguish the two categories by the terms, preference visas and non-preference visas.

The United States **preference system** for immigrant visas is sometimes called a "numbers game." That is because the law establishes the total number of foreign persons who will be admitted to the United States for permanent residence. In order to understand the system of immigrant visas, it is important to understand how the "numbers game" works.

The current law sets a worldwide limit of 700,000 persons that may be admitted as permanent residents to the United States. Of these 700,000 visas, every nation is limited to a yearly maximum of permanent visas for family sponsored and employment related visas which cannot exceed seven per cent of the total number of visas made available in that fiscal year. Dependent areas such as St. Kitts, Nevis, etc. are limited to two per cent of the yearly limit.

Hong Kong is treated separately under the current law and is considered an independent country for permanent visa allocation. For the years 1991 through 1993 the total number of family-sponsored and employment related visas cannot exceed 10,000. However, for years 1991 through 1993 an additional 12,000 visas annually are made available to certain employees of United States businesses.

Generally, the place of birth of the alien determines the country to which he/she will be charged for immigration purposes. There are, however special rules which allow the immigration authorities the right to charge the aliens' spouse's or child's home country with the immigration number rather than the alien himself in order to provide for a family unity.

One way to visualize the worldwide numerical limitations quota is to imagine a long line of persons attempting to enter the Unites States. In order to get to the immigration counter to have his visa application considered on its merits, each person has to take a number and wait on line. In our metaphor, the "number" on the line is the priority date. That is the date on which the alien's visa petition or application was accepted as complete. When the alien's priority date is reached his immigrant petition will be considered on its merits. It is this waiting period that we refer to when we speak of the backlog, or delay, in the annual numerical limitations quota. If, for instance, there were a three-year backlog for persons coming to perform labor, only persons who filed petitions or labor certifications three years earlier would be eligible for admission to the United States. In addition, people from certain countries may have an even longer waiting list because their home country may have already exceeded its annual limitation. At the time of the writing of this book, those countries with waiting lists longer than the worldwide quota include: Philippines, Mexico, India, China, Dominican Republic, and dependent areas such as Hong Kong, St. Kitts, Nevis and Antigua.

Thus, not everyone who seeks to immigrate to the United States is eligible. The law established certain categories ("**preferences**") of persons who may enter the United States by way of this annual worldwide limitations quota and establishes other categories of persons who may enter without regard to the numerical limitations quota. Entry to the United States is based upon qualitative and quantitative restrictions, all of which are scrupulously regulated by the immigration authorities.

The following sub-section will discuss the preference system of permanent visas.

2.1 - THE NUMERICAL PREFERENCE/QUOTA SYSTEM. As stated in the beginning of this chapter, most foreign persons seeking to enter the United States as permanent residents or immigrants are subject to a worldwide annual quota of 700,000 persons unless they are also in one of those special categories discussed in the previous chapter.

The law establishes four "**preferences**" of **family-sponsored** immigrants and five preferences of **employment-related** preferences. The annual limitation or quota for family sponsored immigration is 460,000. Of this number, the law establishes that a minimum of 226,000 visas is reserved for distribution among the four preference categories which will be discussed below. The annual limitation or quota for employment related visas is 140,000. This combined total of 366,000 for all preference categories is substantially higher than the former total annual quota of 270,000. The following sections discuss the principal qualifications and conditions of each of these preferences.

2.2 - FAMILY-SPONSORED IMMIGRANTS. The law establishes four preferences for persons who are eligible for permanent immigrant visas to the United States based upon family relationships. The total number of visas for Family-Sponsored Immigrants is 465,000 for the years 1992 through 1994. Starting in 1995 the total number of visas under this category is expanded to 480,000 visas. These annual numerical limitations represent the total number of visas issued to all immigrants based upon family relationships, including immediate relatives of United States citizens. Remember that immediate relatives of U.S. citizens are not counted under the family-sponsored preference category. The number of family-sponsored preference visas is set at a minimum of 226,000. So, in fact, the total number of family-sponsored preference visas could rise above the 226,000 minimum if a large number of immediate relative petitions were filed in any given year. The formula for determining the exact number of family-sponsored preference visas is somewhat complex, but for purposes of this book it is sufficient to understand that the total number of family-sponsored preference visas is now considerably higher than it was previously.

2.2.1 - FAMILY SPONSORED PREFERENCES - FIRST PREFERENCE: UNMARRIED SONS AND DAUGHTERS OF U.S. CITIZENS.

The first preference is comprised of persons who are the unmarried sons and daughters of U.S. citizens. This preference is allotted 23,000 visas annually. An unmarried son or daughter is defined differently under the law than a "child," since a "child" is defined under the law as an unmarried person under the age of twenty one years (21). Thus, a "child" of a U.S. citizen would be a son or daughter of a U.S. citizen who is under the age of twenty one years and is unmarried, and consequently is entitled to enter the United States without regard to the numerical limitations formula. This is a category of limited application and of limited demand, and, as a result, is not backlogged on the worldwide quota. In the language of the immigration regimen, this preference is considered "current," and anyone who qualifies may make an immediate application for an immigrant visa.

2.2.2 - FAMILY SPONSORED PREFERENCES - SECOND PREFERENCE: SPOUSES AND UNMARRIED SONS AND DAUGHTERS OF LAWFUL PERMANENT RESIDENT ALIENS.

This preference pertains to spouses and unmarried sons and daughters of lawful permanent resident aliens. This preference is different from the **First Preference** described above because the **Second Preference** benefits certain relatives of permanent residents as opposed to U.S. citizens. Please note that the term "unmarried son or daughter" is different from the definition of child, and in order to comply under this preference, the son or daughter must be unmarried at the time of the application for the visa, though the person may be of any age. This preference is allotted a minimum total of 114,200 visas. Furthermore, at least 77% of such visas are to be allocated to spouses and children of permanent residents. The other 23% of the total number of visas under this preference is allocated to the unmarried sons or daughters of permanent residents. A divorced son or daughter will qualify under this preference.

If a permanent resident alien of the United States marries a foreign person, then the U.S. resident's foreign spouse will not receive his/her immigrant visa and will not be permitted to enter the United States until his or her priority date is current. Thus, after the marriage takes place, the permanent resident alien's spouse would file an immigration petition for the foreign spouse, and the foreign spouse would have to remain abroad until his or her priority date became current. If the foreign spouse were already in the United States, there is no assurance that the Immigration and Naturalization Service would permit the spouse to remain in the U.S. until the priority date became current. The current law provides an additional 4000 visas to this category, so it is anticipated that the current backlog for this category of visa will improve only slightly.

2.2.3 - FAMILY SPONSORED PREFERENCES - THIRD PREFERENCE: MARRIED SONS AND DAUGHTERS OF UNITED STATES CITIZENS.

This preference provides for a total of 23,400 visas, plus any visas that have not been used by the first two family-sponsored preference groups. The third preference benefits qualified persons who are the married sons or daughters of United States citizens. This third preference should be distinguished from the first preference, which, as already explained, applies to unmarried adult sons and daughters of United States citizens. This preference, as of the writing of this book, was almost current on a worldwide basis, and is expected to remain so in the foreseeable future.

2.2.4 - FOURTH PREFERENCE: BROTHERS AND SISTERS OF UNITED STATES CITIZENS.

The fourth preference provides for a total of 65,000 visas, or 24% of the worldwide annual quota plus any visas that have not been utilized by the first three family-sponsored preference groups, and it benefits qualified persons who are the siblings (brothers and sisters) of United States citizens. The citizen petitioner must be at least 21 years of age in order to file a petition on behalf of the sibling. Half brothers and half sisters are entitled to the benefits of this preference, as long as the sibling relationship was created before both of the siblings were twenty-one years of age.

As a result of the relatively wide-spread eligibility standard of this visa, there is a long waiting list for this visa preference. In the language of Immigration law it is heavily "over-subscribed". In fact, it is so over-subscribed that the actual waiting list for a new petitioner based upon the current rate of advancement of this preference is probably over fifteen years. This is because advancement of the priority date does not coincide with the normal advancement of the calendar. Over the last few years, the priority date for this preference has advanced on average about one week per actual calendar month.

Many United States citizens, in order to benefit their brothers and sisters, might almost routinely file an immigrant visa petition for their foreign siblings, on the basis that at some unspecified future time their brothers or sisters may wish to immigrate permanently to the United States. This action can result in an unfortunate trap, since the foreign sibling may be unable to obtain a temporary non-immigrant visa to the United States as a result of the filing of the family-sponsored third preference petition by the sibling in the United States. This is because the filing of the immigrant visa petition establishes that the foreign person has an intention to reside in the United States on a permanent basis, and this intention, of course, conflicts with the temporary intent required for any one of the various non-immigrant visas, even the B-2 visitor visa.

When the foreign sibling is a business person who may need to come to the United States on temporary business and does not already have a B-visa, it is probably better to avoid filing the fourth preference petition unless the foreign person already has a valid B-visa in his passport. Otherwise the foreign sibling may have, as a condition to obtaining his B-visa, to convince the U.S. consul in the home country that he or she intends to return to the foreign country after each visit to the United States and presently has the intent of visiting the U.S. only on a temporary basis.

While it may seem logical that a foreign person who has a fourth preference petition filed on his behalf, which has at least a seven or eight year waiting period, would still have an intent to return to his home country after a short visit to the United States, the U.S. consular authorities may require some special proof or documentation before granting a temporary visa to the foreign person.

2.3 - EMPLOYMENT-BASED IMMIGRANTS.

IMMACT90 replaced the old third and sixth preference categories with five main categories of employment-based immigrants. The total number of employment-based immigrant visas is 140,000, annually, plus any unused family-sponsored immigrant visas during the previous fiscal year. The employment-based categories are as follows:

2.3.1 EMPLOYMENT BASED FIRST PREFERENCE - PRIORITY WORKERS.

There are 40,000 visas annually available under this category. This preference category encompasses persons of extraordinary ability in the arts and sciences, in the field of education, business or professional athletics, including multinational executives or managers who will work in the United States for the same multinational employer. The high level of achievement that is required by this preference category is demonstrated by sustained national or international acclaim which must be extensively documented. The alien must be seeking to enter the United States to continue work in the field of endeavor which is the subject of the acclaim and the alien's presence and activities must be of benefit to the United States.

An alien qualifies as an outstanding professor or researcher if he/she has received international acclaim in a particular academic field, has at least three years of experience in teaching or research in the field and seeks to enter the United States for a tenured or tenure-track teaching or research position. The position can be for a University or other educational institution or for a private employer, so long as the employer has at least three other persons employed full-time in research.

Evidence that the professor/researcher is recognized internationally requires at least two of the following:

1. Receipt of major international prizes or awards for outstanding achievement in academic field;

2. Membership in academic associations requiring outstanding achievements;

3. Published materials and professional publications written by others about the alien's work;

4. Participation on a panel, or as an individual, judging work of others;

5. Original scientific/scholarly research contribution; or,

6. Authorship of scholarly books or articles.

In order to qualify as a multinational executive or manager under this preference, the alien, during the three years preceding the application, must have been employed for at least one year by a firm or other business entity and seeking to enter the United States in order to continue rendering services to the same employer/firm in a managerial or executive capacity. The definition of "executive" and "manager" is identical with the definition of those terms under the L-1 visa rules. This preference category represents an excellent planning opportunity for those who qualify. There is no particular limitation as to the size of the company or its gross business volume.

IMMACT90 redefines the terms "managerial capacity" and "executive capacity" for both the immigrant visa and the L-1 intracompany transferee non-immigrant visa category. In order to be qualified as a manager, a person must:

1. Manage a corporation, department, subdivision or function;

2. Supervise and control the work of other supervisory, professional, or managerial employees, or else manage an "essential function";

3. Have the authority to make personnel decisions as to hiring and termination, or else function at a "senior level";

4. Exercise discretion over the day to day operations of the activity or function for which he/she has authority. Please note that first-line supervisors are excluded from the statutory definition of a manager, "unless the employees supervised are professional".

Thus, a manager includes persons who manage a function as well as other people. The term "executive capacity" is also redefined as follows:

1. The person must manage an organization or major component or function;

2. Has the authority to establish goals and policies;

3. Has wide latitude and discretionary decision making;

4. Receives only general supervision from higher executives, board of directors or stockholders.

The above definitions encompass executives who also perform tasks necessary to produce the product or provide the service offered by the organization as would be the case with a person who also is a professional, such as an engineer or architect. This subcategory would permit an owner of a business enterprise to immigrate to the United States so long as he would otherwise satisfy the substantive eligibility requirements described above. In a situation in which the prospective employee was also an owner of the enterprise which would hire him, the Immigration and Naturalization Service will scrutinize the petition very closely to discourage fraud. A specific job offer is not required for issuance of this visa, even though it is expected that the alien is coming to perform valuable services for a business entity. It should be assumed that this subcategory will be heavily sought after by foreign persons and will be subject to administrative efforts to curtail its use, followed by judicial interpretation thereof.

Section 2.3.2 - EMPLOYMENT BASED SECOND PREFERENCE - ALIENS OF EXCEPTIONAL ABILITY.

This preference benefits aliens with:

1. Advanced degrees or their equivalent in professional fields;

2. Exceptional ability in the sciences, arts or business.

In order to establish the first status described above, the alien must submit an official academic record showing that he/she has a United States advanced degree or a foreign equivalent degree; or a United States baccalaureate degree or a foreign equivalent degree and documentation from current or former employers stating that the alien has at least five years of progressive post-baccalaureate experience in the specialty.

In order to establish exceptional ability in the sciences, arts or business, the second status mentioned above, the alien must document at least three of the following:

(a) An official academic record showing that the alien has a degree, diploma, certificate, or similar award from a college, university, school, or other institution of learning relating to the area of exceptional ability;

(b) Evidence in the form of letter(s) from current or former employer(s) showing that the alien has at least ten years of full-time experience in the occupation for which he/she is being sought;

(c) A license to practice the profession or certification for a particular profession or occupation;

(d) Evidence that the alien has commanded a salary, or other payment for services, which demonstrates exceptional ability;

(e) Evidence of membership in a professional association; or

(f) Evidence of recognition for achievements and significant contributions to the industry or field by peers, governmental entities, or professional or business organizations.

The INS has indicated that it will consider comparable evidence which is appropriate to the alien's application.

For this preference category, a job offer is required unless the Immigration Service waives that requirement in the national interest. A labor certification is required even for alien who holds an advanced degree (or equivalent). The new law allows a person to have the equivalent of an advanced degree if that person has at least five years progressive experience in the profession beyond the Bachelor's degree. Persons who have exceptional ability in business, however, will still be required to obtain a labor certification. It is important to note that the possession of a degree, diploma, certificate or similar award from a college, university, school or other institution is not sufficient evidence of exceptional ability by itself. Thus, there must be something beyond the basic qualification in a field of endeavor in order for a person to qualify as having exceptional ability.

Section 2.3.3 EMPLOYMENT BASED THIRD PREFERENCE - SKILLED AND UNSKILLED WORKERS.

This preference is a general category that includes all other aliens who are entering the United States with an offer of employment. This category also has 40,000 visas annually plus any of the unused visas from the first two employment based preferences. This category requires a job offer from an employer as well as a labor certification from the U.S. Department of Labor. The subject of labor certification is discussed further on in this chapter. The preference contains three sub-categories:

1. Skilled Workers, defined as aliens capable of performing a job requiring at least two years training or experience;

2. Professionals with a Bachelor's Degree (only);

3. Other workers, also referred to unskilled workers, who are capable of filing positions requiring less than two years training or experience. Only 10,000 of the 40,000 annual visas in the third preference are available to unskilled workers and as a result of this limitation, this writer predicts that the waiting time for this category will be very long. IMMACT90 90 is obviously geared toward bringing in skilled workers for the economy and against bringing in unskilled workers.

The segregation of these two sub-preferences from each other prevents the category for skilled workers from becoming as backlogged as the category for unskilled workers.

Section 2.3.4 - FOURTH PREFERENCE - SPECIAL IMMIGRANTS (INCLUDING RELIGIOUS WORKERS)

This preference category is allocated 10,000 visas annually plus any left over visas from the higher employment based categories. Included in this category are religious workers. In order to qualify, the religious worker must have been a member of and working for the religious organization for at least two years, and be seeking to enter the United

States to:

1. Be a minister of religion;

2. Work for the organization in a professional capacity in a religious vocation;

3. Work for the organization or a related, tax-exempt entity in some other non-professional capacity in a religious vocation or occupation.

Aliens who seek to work in a professional capacity must have at least a baccalaureate degree in order to qualify for this visa. This requirement does not apply to a minister of religion.

Only 5,000 of the 10,000 annual limit of these visas may be used by religious workers and both of the above mentioned religious worker sub-categories will terminate on October 1, 1994.

Employees at U.S. Consulate in Hong Kong - This special visa category has 500 visas. The first 500 visas under this category will not be counted against any numerical limitation. These provisions will be available to employees at the U.S. Consulate in Hong Kong up to January 1, 2002. In order to qualify, the employee must have performed faithful service for at least three years.

Certain Juveniles: A third sub-group of special immigrants are aliens who have been declared dependent on a juvenile court and for whom it has been decided that it is not in their best interest to be returned to their homeland. The natural parents of such aliens are unable to derive any Immigration benefits simply because their child has gained special immigrant status.

Section 2.3.5 INVESTORS/EMPLOYMENT CREATION.

This employment based preference category contains 10,000 visas per year for foreign investors. This is a fixed number and does not benefit from any unused visas in any of the other employment based preferences. The investment requirement ranges from a low of $500,000.00 invested in a rural area or of high unemployment up to $3,000,000.00 in an enterprise located in a region of the country that is deemed to be of low unemployment. The alien must have invested the money after November 29, 1990 or be in the active process of investing the money. The supplementing rules and regulations have only recently been promulgated but the investment must create at least ten full time jobs for U.S. citizens, permanent resident aliens or other immigrants lawfully authorized to be employed in the United States. This group of ten workers provided for by the law cannot include the investor or his/her immediate family.

The law encourages investment in areas of high unemployment or other areas known as "targeted employment areas" and those areas are defined as rural areas or areas having an unemployment rate at least 1 1/2 times the national average. If the investment is made in a "targeted employment area" then only five jobs must be created, and the investments can be as low as $500,000.00. Of the 10,000 annual visas in this preference category 3000 are reserved for "targeted employment areas".

As of the date of writing of this book, the Immigration and Naturalization Service had implemented only the provision for the investment of $1,000.000.00 on a "wait and see" approach to determine how and if it would implement the provisions for the investment of the $500,000.00 sum in areas of high unemployment. In order to implement the application of the $500,000.00 amount with its concomitant employment creation of five jobs, it will be necessary for the individual states to designate, subject to federal government approval, which geographic areas or political subdivisions in which the lesser investment amount will be authorized in order to garner the benefits of this visa program. As of the date of the writing of this book only one state and the Commonwealth of Puerto Rico had set up a mechanism for determining areas of high unemployment.

The law provides a number of measures to deter fraud by immigrant investors, with fines of up to $250,000.00 and jail for up to five years. In addition, the law also makes the grant of permanent residence to immigrant investors conditional and has established a two year trial period. During this two year period, by rule and regulation, the Immigration and Naturalization Service will determine whether the enterprise is created to evade U.S. immigration laws, whether or not the enterprise was, in fact, established, whether or not the capital was, in fact, invested, or whether the alien did not sustain the enterprise. Within ninety days prior to the end of the two year period, the investor must file an additional petition or paper with the Immigration and Naturalization Service requesting that the conditional status of residence be removed.

The administrative regulations published by the Immigration and Naturalization Service provide that a qualified investment includes the purchase of an existing business so long as the enterprise' worth, after the completion of the sale, is at least 140% of the value of the enterprise prior to the date of the acquisition. This requirement will prevent an investor from merely purchasing an ongoing business without causing any substantive improvement in the capital or employment levels of the enterprise. In addition, the regulations provide for the purchase and overhaul of a troubled or undercapitalized business enterprise by a foreign person. This feature is very interesting because most business consultants agree that it is usually preferable to purchase an ongoing business enterprise rather than for a person to attempt the development of a new business--in a foreign country.

This visa requires that the investor manage the business personally and does not anticipate that the investor be merely a passive financier, unless the investor is a limited partner in a limited partnership formed in accordance with the requirements of a certain uniform limited partnership law. The provision for the limited partner is contradictory to the requirement that the investor directly manage and/or supervise the investment. This is because the limited partnership act referred to, by its very terms, defines the limited partner as a passive investor. Since a limited partnership interest is a security and will support an employment creation investor visa, one wonders why the INS regulations do not also permit other types of securities to provide a permanent visa as long as the requisite level of employment is created.

CONDITIONAL GRANT OF VISA: This visa will be issued, initially, for a period of two years, after which time, if the investment is still in place, the visa will be permanent and no longer subject to the investor's continued personal involvement in the enterprise. This visa is quite appropriate for the acquisition of hotel/motel properties especially in resort or tourist areas where the real estate can be expected to retain its value. It is the author's personal view that foreign persons should favor the more conservative approach to investment in the United States until they have developed insight into the economy and business customs of the location in which they are investing. Real estate investments, including hotels and motels, generally fit into this mold.

One warning that I offer is that by becoming a permanent resident of the United States, the foreign person becomes a United States taxpayer and thus subjects his worldwide income to taxation. Proper pre-investment planning is absolutely essential in order to avoid fiscal disasters; and a foreign investor should consult a tax professional, both abroad as well as in the United States to assist in the various phases of the investment. This is discussed in the section on taxation starting on page 93 of this book.

Section 2.3.6 HONG KONG RESIDENT/EMPLOYEES OF U.S. BUSINESSES. The law authorizes the issuance of up to 12,000 immigrant visas in fiscal years 1991, 1992 and 1993 to certain employees of United States businesses operating in Hong Kong as well as the spouses and children of such aliens, if they accompany or plan to join the employee. In order to be eligible, the alien must have been a resident of Hong Kong and must have been employed in a managerial executive capacity or one involving specialized knowledge within the previous consecutive twelve months. In order to qualify for one of these visas, the alien employee must:

1. Have been employed as an officer or supervisor, or in a managerial, executive or specialized knowledge capacity;

2. Have an immediate offer of employment from a U.S. company in the same capacity, and at a comparable salary and benefit to other similarly situated employees. The business must be owned or organized in the United States or be an affiliate or subsidiary of such a business and it must employ at least 100 persons in the United States and at least 50 employees outside the United States, though not necessarily in Hong Kong, and they must have a gross annual income of at least $50,000,000.00. The definition of manager and executive is the same as has been previously explained in Section 2.7.2., and the definition of specialized knowledge includes specialized knowledge of the company's product and its application in international markets, or an advanced level of knowledge of the company's processes and procedures. The law defines "officer" for purposes of the special Hong Kong provision to include the Chairman or Vice-Chairman of the Board of Directors, the President and the Vice-President or Assistant Vice-President and any trust officer or controllers, several other job titles and any other officer of the entity customarily performing similar functions (Section 1.2.4(d)(3)). The term supervisor is also defined and includes any individual having authority to hire, fire, recall, promote or undertake similar personnel functions, as long as the exercise of this authority, requires independent judgment is not merely routine or clerical. The above definitions are very generous to Hong Kong employees and afford employees of U.S./Hong Kong companies more liberalized definitions which allow them to qualify more easily than similar employees of companies from other countries.

The petition to take advantage of this provision must be filed with the Immigration and Naturalization Regional Service Center having jurisdiction over the petitioner's United States corporate headquarters. The listing of the Regional Service Centers is included as an Appendix to this book. The law also allows natives of Hong Kong to delay entering the United States once they have received the permanent visa. Other aliens must enter the United States within four months of receiving an immigrant visa or else it is deemed to be abandoned. But Hong Kong residents can delay entry into the U.S. under the terms of their permanent visas until January 1, 2002, at which time they must still be eligible for admission.

In accordance with the logic of the immigration system, it is the U.S. employer who is the moving party in the visa petition. The employee is the beneficiary of the system and basically has no rights until the government actually issues the visa. This point is made clearer in the discussion of the labor certification process below.

2.4 - THE LABOR CERTIFICATION PROCESS.

As explained previously, the second, third and fourth Employment Based Preferences require as a pre-condition that the foreign person receive a "labor certification" from the Department of Labor. The labor certification is, in essence, a finding that there are not enough qualified workers in the United States location where the foreign person will perform his job or services and that the employment of the alien will not adversely affect the United States labor market. In practical terms, this means that an employer will offer a position to a foreign person and will employ that foreign person if the Department of Labor approves the employment.

The requirements for receiving a job certification from the Department of Labor are burdensome. First, the processing time for the labor certification, which is a prerequisite to filing the second and third employment-based visa petitions, can be one year or more in length. In addition to the job certification delay, the alien must still wait for the "priority date" to become current for the visa itself. The alien cannot file the immigrant visa petition until the Labor Certification has been approved. Then, there is a backlog or delay as to visa availability. The waiting period for visas for unskilled workers has been, as of the writing of this book, about three and a half (3 1/2) years. The person, however, receives his priority date on the day that his labor certification request is received for processing.

The application for the job certification is filed on a form known as Form ETA 750 which is comprised of two parts: Part A and Part B. Part A is filled out by the employer and lists the employer's requirements, while Part B is filled out by the employee and lists the employee's qualifications.

The process is initiated when the employer offers the alien a job and then files an application for a labor certification with the U.S. Department of Labor. The initial filing is with the local state labor office which processes and transmits the same together with its recommendations to the regional U.S. Department of Labor office.

In order to obtain a labor certification, the employer must prove to the Department of Labor that the job being offered to the alien is available and is otherwise open to persons in the United States, and that there are no unreasonable or unnecessary conditions placed on the position. In the United States, a job requirement that a person must speak a particular foreign language is considered unreasonable on its face and can only be overcome by proof that knowledge of a foreign language is essential to the proper performance of the job. The employer must also prove that it has made a reasonable effort to fill that position with U.S. citizens or permanent residents. The employer is required to advertise the position in a newspaper of general circulation, sometimes in a professional or trade journal, and must post on his place of employment information concerning the availability of that position.

In order to fully appreciate the philosophy of the Department of Labor and Immigration and Naturalization Service with respect to the issuance of "labor certification"(s), the following quotation from the FEDERAL REGISTER concerning the Employment Based second and third preferences is instructive:

"THE LABOR CERTIFICATION PROCESS BRIEFLY DESCRIBED - Generally, an individual labor certification from the Department is required for employers wishing to employ an alien under Preference Groups 2 and 3. In issuing such certifications, DOL applies two basic standards to exclude an alien:(1) if U.S. workers are able, willing, qualified and available for the position; and /or(2) if the employment of an alien will adversely affect the wages or working conditions of U.S. workers similarly employed.

In brief, the current process for obtaining a labor certification requires employers to actively recruit U.S. workers in good faith for a period of at least thirty days for the job openings for which aliens are sought. The employers' job requirements must be reasonable and realistic, and employers must offer prevailing wages and working conditions for the occupation. The employers may not favor aliens or tailor the job requirements to the aliens' qualifications.

During the thirty-day recruitment period, employers are required to place a three-day, help wanted advertisement in a newspaper of general circulation, or a one-day advertisement in a professional, trade or business journal, or ethnic publication. Employers are also required to place a thirty-day job order with the local office of the State employment service. If employers believe they have already conducted adequate recruitment, they may ask the Department to waive the mandatory, thirty-day recruitment. It the employer does not request a waiver of recruitment or if the waiver request is denied, the help-wanted advertisements which are placed in conjunction with the mandatory thirty-day recruitment direct job applicants to either report in person to the employment service or to submit resumes to the employment service.

The job applicants are then referred to the employer or their resumes are sent. The employer then has forty-five days to report to the employment service the job-related reasons for not hiring any U.S. workers referred. If the employer hires a U.S. worker for the job opening, the process stops at that point, unless the employer has more than one opening. If, however, the employer believes that qualified, willing and able U.S. workers are not available to take the job, the application together with the documentation of the recruitment results and prevailing wage information are sent to the regional office of DOL [Department of Labor]. There, it is reviewed and a determination is made as to whether or not to issue the labor certification..."

The above explanation means the Department of Labor will deny the labor certification if the employer requires special conditions that only a foreign person can or is willing to fulfill, unless those conditions are essential to his business. So, a requirement that the person holding the job speak a foreign language will disqualify the labor certification unless the employer can prove that the foreign language requirement is an essential part of the job. Mere convenience or slight competitive advantage to an employer is not sufficient. Also, the employer must offer the prevailing wage for that job that is paid in the community and must not impose higher than normal education or experience requirements for the position.

Obviously, the Department of Labor wants to ensure that an employer does not bypass available U.S. workers so that the employer can give the job to an alien of his choice. The labor certification process can be long and arduous, and very often places considerable administrative burdens on the employer as well as personal and financial strains and risks on the employee.

While the particular job market, based upon economic and labor conditions prevalent in the area of intended employment, will determine the feasibility of obtaining a labor certification, certain trends are apparent. First, it is generally easier to obtain a labor certification for job skills which occupy the opposite ends of the spectrum with respect to job complexity. Thus, a scientist who is experienced in advanced molecular bio-chemistry will probably receive a labor certification. Likewise, an attendant for a coin operated laundry at the prevailing wage for that position may also be approved for labor certification. That is because in both instances, the prospective employer may not be able to find a qualified U.S. worker to fill the position, either because of the high degree of training and experience required or because of the poor job description and low wages offered. In both cases, the result is the same in that the employer is unable to fill the job position.

Thus, the economy and the law favor persons who have particular job capabilities and skills that are not readily obtainable in the U.S. labor market. An employer who wishes to hire a foreign person who possesses only general administrative and sales skills will find it very difficult to obtain the required labor certification. Of course, in particular circumstances it is advisable to consult with a qualified immigration attorney who is familiar with the job market in the area of intended employment.

Problem of Intent (Again). As a result of filing the immigrant visa petition, an alien may find that his ability to travel to the United States can be curtailed. This could happen in at least two typical circumstances: First, the U.S. consulate in the foreign country may not grant a temporary visa to the alien; or secondly, if the alien already has a valid temporary visa to the United States, the alien's right to travel to the United States under the temporary visa may be challenged by the Immigration Inspector at the port of entry. In this latter case, the INS may interview the alien to determine whether he is still entitled to use the temporary visa for entry to the United States. In some extreme cases, the INS may not allow the person to enter the United States at all, and, thus, will turn him away at the border.

This problem is caused by the requirement of the law that the alien's intent as to his/her duration of stay be consistent with the type of visa that the alien holds. If the alien has filed a petition for permanent residency, she or he has stated, in effect, that his or her intent is to remain in the U.S. on a permanent basis. Thus, the INS may decide that the alien is ineligible to receive or use a non-immigrant (temporary) visa since these visas require that the alien have an intention to remain in the U.S. for a temporary period only. This problem of intent can present a most unfortunate surprise. So, an alien who wishes to travel to the United States on a temporary visit should not file the petition for permanent residency until his temporary visit has been concluded.

If the alien is already in the United States, the filing of a permanent visa petition may disqualify him/her from extending or renewing his temporary visa or the duration of stay under the temporary visa.

2.5 - SPECIAL PROBLEM: LIVE-IN DOMESTIC WORKERS. The United States does not look kindly on live-in domestic workers. The Department of Labor acknowledges there is a shortage of live-in domestic workers, but not live-out domestic workers. It is a characteristic of U.S. society that domestic workers generally are not willing to live in the household of their employers, at least not without requiring a premium in wages.

In order to obtain an immigrant visa as a live-in domestic worker the alien must prove by documentation that she or he has had twelve months of paid experience in the capacity of a domestic worker abroad. However, the most difficult part of a live-in domestic worker application is the requirement that the employer prove there is an absolute "business necessity" for employing a live-in domestic. Normally, an employer must show there are no adults at home who could take care of either young children or if an adult who may require constant attention, and that the employers' job occupations require frequent travel away from the home. The Department of Labor will go to great lengths to suggest alternatives to employers as to how to rearrange their lives, so as not to require a live-in domestic worker. The difficulty in obtaining the labor certification, together with the over-burdened third preference for unskilled workers results in long delays in obtaining a visa based upon employment as a live-in domestic worker. As of the writing of this book the waiting period was approximately three and one half years. This long delay makes it very difficult to secure a position and thus enter the United States as an immigrant on this basis.

2.6 - SPECIAL PROBLEM - INVESTORS (Other than those who qualify for the new Employment Creation visa).

A business entrepreneur could technically qualify under a second or third employment based preference visa, except that he/she must be entering the United States as an employee. The obvious suggestion comes to mind that perhaps the investor could form a company in the United States that would hire him. While this is technically possible, in the practical world, it is very difficult to achieve.

The investor must compete with U.S. job seekers for the position he seeks to fill himself. The Department of Labor has taken a very negative attitude about permitting an investor to evaluate applicants who are competing with the investor for the position. The United States Department of Labor is obviously concerned that the investor may not be impartial or objective in his analysis. The Department of Labor will require that the investor prove that the labor certification selection process is conducted by objective persons who are independent from the influence of the investor. If the Department of Labor determines that the employee for whom the labor certification is sought is the principal or is one of the principal investors in a company, it will routinely deny the labor certification. As a result, the investor has the burden of establishing the objectivity of the selection process. Under the circumstances described this would be an almost impossible burden. There have been instances in which an investor holding a small minority of stock, generally no more that five (5%) percent, has been certified for the position sought. These circumstances are rare, however, and I would advise such an applicant not to invest in the company in which he is seeking employment. It would be preferable to obtain an option to purchase stock in the future based upon job performance rather than have to meet the burden of proving to the Department of Labor that the investor, as a result of his/her minority ownership of stock, will not be in a position to unduly influence the selection process of workers for the position which he is also seeking.

2.7 - OCCUPATIONS FOR WHICH LABOR CERTIFICATION IS NOT REQUIRED.

The law identifies a group of occupations which are presumed to be in demand in the United States and for which no labor certification is required. These occupations are designated under "Schedule A," and there are two (2) groups of persons who, upon proof of their qualifications, do not need to obtain a labor certification before applying for an immigrant visa. These groups are as follows:

Group I - Physical therapists, and professional nurses. Physical therapist is defined in the law as follows:

"A person who applies the art and science of physical therapy to the treatment of patients' disability disorders, and injuries to relieve pain, develop or restore function, and maintain performance, using physical means such as exercise, massage, heat, water, light, and electricity as prescribed by a physician (or surgeon)."
(20 CFR 656.10a4 I)

"to prove eligibility for this group, the alien must have all the qualifications necessary to take the licensing examination in the state in which he intends to practice physical therapy. Thus, the alien must file, together with his application, a letter or statement signed by an authorized licensing official in the state of intended employment stating that the alien is qualified to take the state's licensing examination for physical therapists".
(20 CFR 656.22 C)

Professional nurses are also exempt from the labor certification requirement, and these are defined as

"persons who apply the art and science of nursing, which reflects comprehension of principles derived from the physical, biological, and behavioral sciences. Professional nursing generally includes the making of judgments concerning the observation, caring, counsel of persons requiring nursing care; and administering of medicines and treatments prescribed by the physician or dentist; the participation in activities for the promotion of health and the prevention of illness in others. A program of study for professional nurses generally includes theory and practice in clinical areas such as: obstetrics, surgery, pediatrics, psychiatry, and medicine."
(20 CFR 656.50)

In addition to the above, the nurse alien must pass the Commission on Graduates of Foreign Nursing Schools Examination, as well as hold a full and unrestricted license to practice professional nursing in the state of intended employment.

Group II - Persons of "*exceptional ability in the sciences or arts, including college and university teachers who have been practicing their science or art during the year before the application.*" The Department of Labor takes the position that the term "exceptional ability" means international reknown.

"Such aliens should be so far above the average members of their fields that they will clearly be an asset to the United States."
(Federal Register, Number 5, 1976)

In order to qualify for this category of skilled worker which will eliminate the requirement of a labor certification application, the alien must file a considerable amount of documentary evidence establishing his international reknown and recognition by recognized experts in the field. The documentation may include the following: internationally recognized prizes or awards, membership in international associations which require outstanding achievement of members, published treatises and materials and professional publication, evidence of the alien's participation on panels or as a judge of the work of others in the same or a similar field of scholarly research, contributions of major significance, evidence of the alien's scholarship and published scientific or scholarly articles, international professional journals, or evidence of the display of the alien's work at artistic exhibitions in more than one country. It must be emphasized that documentation is critical, and any alien who feels he might qualify for admission to the United States under this exception must accumulate as much detailed documentation as to his credentials as is possible. It is doubtful that such an application could be presented properly without the assistance of an attorney who specializes in immigration law, but even when an attorney is used, the considerable documentation described is indispensable.

2.8 - DIVERSITY IMMIGRANTS

Starting October 1, 1994, in addition to immigrants entering the United States based upon marital or family relationships and entry based upon employment sponsored visas, a new so-called "diversity" immigrant visa will be available. 55,000 visas per year will be made available for diversity immigrants and their family members on a lottery type basis.

These visas will be made available to persons who are nationals of "low admission" countries. The prospective immigrant must have at least a high school equivalent education or equivalent, or have worked at least two years in an occupation that requires two years of training or experience. The law (IMMACT90) divides the world into six regions and then establishes a formula for determining which region and which state qualifies as high or low admission. In the recent past, the greatest number of immigrants to the United States have come from Asia and Latin America, with a smaller number coming from Europe and Africa. The purpose of the Diversity Immigrant visa is to provide a separate entry basis for those persons who come from low admission regions and states. It is beyond the scope of this book to go into the details of the mathematical formula which is used to determine low and high admission areas. While the number and identification of the regions and states will vary from year to year, it is safe to assume that those countries that presently have high admissions into the United States will continue to be, at least for the near term, high admission countries in the future and thus, the nationals of those countries would be excluded from participating in the diversity program. Those countries would probably be as follows, but the countries will change:

> Canada, Colombia, Dominican Republic, El Salvador, Haiti, India, Jamaica, Korea, Mexico, Peoples Republic of China, Philippines, Taiwan and the United Kingdom.

2.9 - THE ROLE OF THE STATE DEPARTMENT

The United States State Department, which operates the Diversity Immigrant Program, will designate a period during which diversity visa petitions or applications must be filed for the next fiscal year. At this time, the State Department regulations have not been issued which would otherwise specify the information which must be included in the petition as well as the supporting documentation. These specific rules will probably change year by year as circumstances warrant.

Each diversity visa applicant can only submit one application in a given year, and if more than one visa application is received from one applicant, it will void all of the applications. It is probable that the Diversity Visa Program will operate similar to a lottery system with a system of random selection of all eligible entries.

2.10 - TRANSITION DIVERSITY PROGRAM

In addition, starting October 1, 1991, and through September 30, 1994, there will be a Transitional Diversity Program under which 40,000 immigrant visas will be issued each year to natives of adversely affected states that participated in a previous lottery program. Natives from the following countries will be able to participate in the Transitional Diversity Program:

Albania, Algeria, Argentina, Austria, Belgium, Bermuda, Canada (recently added), Czechoslovakia, Denmark, Estonia, Finland, France, Germany, Gibraltar, Great Britain and Northern Ireland, Guadeloupe, Hungary, Iceland, Indonesia, Ireland, Italy, Japan, Latvia, Liechtenstein, Lithuania, Luxembourg, Monaco, New Caledonia, Netherlands, Norway, Poland, San Marino, Sweden, Switzerland and Tunisia.

As a result of strong political influence from a well known member of the U.S. Senate, the 1990 Immigration Act requires that at least 40% of the 40,000 visas issued during this transitional period shall go to natives of Ireland and their spouses and children.

The Transitional Diversity Program also requires that the successful applicant have a firm commitment of employment in the U.S. valid for a period of at least one year after admission. Obviously, this benefits those who are already in the United States as they will be able to find a job offer more easily than someone living abroad. The requirement is that a person must provide a "letter from an bonafide employer communicating their willingness to hire the alien". In addition, the alien cannot have any of the exclusion disabilities which would otherwise keep a person from entering the United States.

NON-PREFERENCE CATEGORIES

2.11 - PERSONS ELIGIBLE TO IMMIGRATE TO THE UNITED STATES WITHOUT REGARD TO THE QUOTA SYSTEM

2.11.a. - <u>IMMEDIATE RELATIVES OF U.S. CITIZENS</u>. The law provides that certain immediate relatives of U.S. citizens may receive permanent visas without regard to the system of numerical limitations. The categories for which this chapter applies are the <u>parents</u>, <u>spouse</u>, or <u>child</u>, of a United States citizen. The philosophy behind this, as well as other categories of the U.S. immigration system is to provide for the maintenance of the unity of the family. It is important to understand, however, that it is the United States citizen who has the right to make a petition to the United States Government requesting that the beneficiary receive a permanent visa. Understanding this simple concept can very often avoid unfortunate consequences, especially for the spouse of a U.S. citizen.

<u>Spouse of a U.S. Citizen.</u> A United States citizen may petition either the Department of Naturalization and Immigration Service or the U.S. Consul abroad for a permanent visa for the alien spouse. The foremost prerequisite under the law for this category is that there must be a valid and subsisting marriage between the parties and that the marriage be recognized under the law of where the marriage took place. The law does not recognize polygamous or proxy marriages, unless, in the latter case, the marriage has been consummated.

The law also does not recognize sham marriages or marriages where the primary purpose is to obtain immigration benefits and where the parties never intended to live together as husband and wife. In addition, the use of a sham marriage to apply for visas is against the law and subjects both parties as well as any other person involved in procuring the visa under these fraudulent conditions to criminal prosecution.

Under the terms of current law, if a marriage is of less than two years duration at the time the petition for the permanent visa is filed, the alien spouse of a U.S. citizen receives only "conditional" permanent resident status. Upon the second anniversary of the granting of the original conditional permanent resident status, the alien may achieve the permanent resident status. The temporary resident status automatically terminates within two years unless the alien and spouse jointly submit a petition within 90 days prior to the end of the twenty four month period requesting the removal of the conditional grant of resident status. It is contemplated that the parties will be interviewed by an immigration officer. If the foreign person fails to file the required form, with supporting documentation, on time, the conditional permanent resident status will be terminated. Late filing of this form will be accepted only upon proof of good cause and extenuating circumstances justifying the late filing. In addition, the conditional status or temporary resident status will be terminated by the attorney general within two years if he determines the following:

a) That the qualifying marriage was entered into for the purpose of obtaining the alien's entry as an immigrant; or

b) That the qualifying marriage has been annulled or terminated, other than through the death of the spouse; or

c) That a fee or other consideration was given for the filing of the petition (other than attorneys fees for assistance in preparing petition).

The major cause for concern by an alien spouse is (b) which states that the Attorney General is authorized to terminate the visa if the marriage has been terminated other than through death. In the event of a termination of a marriage prior to the expiration of the two year period, it is possible that an alien may obtain a waiver with respect to the consequences imposed by the fact that the marriage was terminated, only if the alien can demonstrate that:

a) Circumstances arose during the period of the conditional permanent residence which would cause extreme hardship if he/she were deported.

b) That the qualifying marriage was entered into in good faith but was terminated for good cause and that the alien was not at fault in failing to meet the requirements ordinarily prescribed for the removal of the condition period.

c) There is also a provision in the law which permits an alien spouse who has been physically battered by her (his) spouse to protect her right to retain permanent residency status without showing that her loss of permanent residency status would cause extreme hardship if he/she were deported. The requirements for proving that the spouse is a "battered spouse" are unrealistic in many circumstances. If an alien spouse feels that he/she cannot continue in the marriage because of physical battery, he/she should consult an immigration attorney as well as a qualified matrimonial lawyer in order to document the battery properly.

However, an alien who obtained lawful permanent residence status as the beneficiary spouse of a U.S. citizen or of a permanent resident alien is, for a period of five years from the date of approval of his/her original immigrant visa petition, unable to confer second preference status on behalf of his/her new spouse -- unless the first marriage was terminated by death. This restriction may be waived if the alien can establish by clear and convincing evidence that the prior marriage was not entered into for the purpose of evading the provision of the Immigration laws.

The most recent immigration law amendments have established a system which will:

1. Automatically identify persons whose marriage fits the profile of a non bona-fide marriage and;

2. Provides for a more objective method of adjudicating the termination of those visas.

Widows and Widowers of U.S. Citizens

IMMACT90 provides that a widow or widower of a U.S. citizen may apply for an immigrant visa as an immediate relative if he/she had been married to the United States citizen for a period of two years prior to the U.S. spouse's death. The deceased spouse must have been a U.S. citizen for at least two years prior to his/her death and the petition must be filed no later than two years following the death of the U.S. citizen. It is also required that the widow/widower not have been legally separated from the United States citizen at the time of the citizen's death. It is difficult to imagine how this requirement will be implemented in the case of those persons who live in states where there is no legal status known as "legally separated". In the state of Florida, with which I am familiar, a marital separation exists when the parties physically or even sexually separate, and there is no particular legal process to determine when the parties have done so. This is one of the peculiarities of the U.S. immigration regimen in that it attempts to establish a defined legal status even though the particular state may not use the same nomenclature or even agree to implement the public policy which motivates the immigration law or regulation.

Until November, 1992, it will not matter what length of time the decedent had been a U.S. citizen. Thus, for any person who had been married to a deceased U.S. citizen which decedent had not been a U.S. citizen for at least two years, the alien widow/widower may, until November, 1992 file the petition for immigrant status. One of the requirements of the INS is that the widow/widower must not have remarried at the time of the petition. The policy reason for this rule is unclear.

NOTE: Normally, an alien does not have a vested right to immigrant status based upon marriage to a U.S. citizen. If the marriage should terminate, whether by divorce or death, prior to the granting of the visa, the alien will have no right to apply for an immigrant visa, except as noted above, regardless of how long he or she has lived in the United States or how deserving the alien may be of obtaining the visa.

Thus, an alien should require that the U.S. citizen spouse file the petition on the alien's behalf as soon as possible after the marriage unless the marriage will soon reach the second anniversary, in which case it is advisable to wait until the two year anniversary in order to avoid the conditional two year visa. All of this discussion presumes that the alien is already in the United States at the time of the marriage.

If the parties are outside of the United States at the time of the marriage, then the alien will not be permitted to enter the United States until the visa petition has been approved at the U.S. consulate abroad. This process may take as long as four months! Therefore, it is advisable to plan the marriage and/or the entry to the U.S. accordingly. Also, if the parties were married in the United States then the alien spouse should not depart the United States until the alien's status has been adjusted to that of a permanent resident alien (immigrant). Again, the mere fact that an alien is married to a U.S. citizen does not convey on the alien the right to enter or remain in the United States prior to receiving an immigrant visa. This simple statement should be thoroughly understood by both the U.S. citizen and alien spouse.

If either spouse has been previously married, it will be necessary to prove the valid termination of the prior marriage(s).

Child of a United States Citizen. The law permits unlimited immigrant visas to persons who qualify as the "child" of United States citizens. "Child" as defined under the law means an <u>unmarried</u> person under the age of twenty-one years of age. If an alien does not qualify under this category as a result of age or marital status he or she may still qualify for an immigrant visa under the First or Fourth Preferences, both of which are covered in this book.

A stepchild is also included within the scope of "child" if the marriage between the natural and step parent occurred prior to the person's eighteenth birthday.

The benefits of the law apply only to legitimate children unless the child was legitimated according to the law and/or a recognized custom of the place of his birth, or unless the mother of the illegitimate child is a U.S. citizen.

An adopted child is also recognized under the law for immediate relative status if the child was adopted prior to his sixteenth birthday and resided with the adopting parents for a minimum period of two years.

An orphan also qualifies if the child was orphaned before attaining sixteen years of age and has been either adopted by the U.S. parents, or single parent who has attained the minimum age of twenty-five years; or if the U.S. parents or parent, as the case may be, have satisfied the U.S. immigration authorities of their intention to adopt the orphan in the United States and that they have qualified for the adoption under law of the state where they intend to live.

Parents of a U.S. Citizen. The third category of the "immediate relative" category, which enables an alien to enter the United States without regard to the numerical quota, benefits the parents of United States citizens. The U.S. citizen, however, must be at least twenty-one years of age in order to give the parent the right of entry under the immigrant visa. The two chief requirements under this section are that the relationship of "parent" and "child" as defined by law must have been established at the time the family relationship was created. Thus, if an alien adopts a United States person over the age of twenty-one the alien will not gain immigration benefits. This is because at the time of the adoption the person adopted was not a "child" as defined under the law. The adopted person was an adult and thus the parent is not the parent of a United States "child". If, however, the U.S. citizen was a "child" at the time of the adoption but is an adult at the time of the filing of the petition the parent may still obtain the benefits of this section since the legal immigration definition of "parent" and "child" were satisfied when the civil relationship was created. Under all of the previous three sections with respect to the immediate relative status, the U.S. citizen must file on behalf of the alien a form I-130, which is a preliminary petition. This form is readily available at all U.S. consulates abroad and all I.N.S. offices in the United States.

2.11.b. - OTHER PERSONS NOT SUBJECT TO THE QUOTA SYSTEM. In addition to the immediate relatives of a U.S. citizen, there are other persons who may enter the United States for permanent residency without the requirement of conforming with the worldwide numerical quota. The first of these, of course, is the permanent resident alien who is returning to the United States from a <u>temporary</u> visit abroad. Thus, the alien must have already been lawfully admitted for permanent residence, and his visit abroad must have been temporary without an intention to abandon his immigrant status in the United States. Usually the immigrant visa ("Green Card") itself is sufficient documentation to enable an alien who has been temporarily abroad to return to the United States.

If the alien is planning to remain outside the United States for a period of one year or more, he should obtain permission from the United States Immigration and Naturalization Service to do so, and this is obtained by filling out an official form. This form, when approved by the Immigration and Naturalization Service, establishes that the alien is not abandoning his permanent residency in the United States even though he may be outside the country for a period of more than one year. Other persons who have special status are certain foreign medical school graduates who obtained certain H or J Visas before January 10, 1978, remained in the United States, and were licensed to practice medicine in the United States on or before January 9. 1978.

Family Members Accompanying to Join. The spouse and child(ren) of the petitioning alien receive a derivative visa which permits them to enter the United States together with the petitioning alien. In immigrant cases this provision of law regards the spouse or child(ren) as accompanying the principal if they receive immigrant visas within four months after the principal obtains an immigrant visa or adjustment of status within the United States or within four months after the principal departs from the home country. In fact, if the principal's family members as defined by law "follow to join" the principal they would be entitled to derivative status at any time after the principal acquires his immigrant visa.

If the relationship of spouse or child is created after the principal has obtained his visa then the family members would not be entitled to the derived permanent visa status. This would be the case if the principal were to marry his spouse after he had acquired his immigrant visa. Also, an accompanying relative may not precede the principal alien to the United States. In either of the above cases the family members would be required to file a separate immigrant visa petition and would be subject to the worldwide numerical limitations quota.

2.12 - ADJUSTMENT OF STATUS. Normally, the permanent visas is issued in a U.S. Consulate abroad. The U.S. Congress has long recognized that for many people who are already in the United States, the necessity of a trip abroad for final processing was both inconvenient and expensive. As a result, a procedure has been created entitled Adjustment Of Status which enables a person in the United States to receive the permanent visa from within the United States. However, there are conditions to this procedure.

First, the person must be eligible to receive a permanent visa immediately. Thus, a person who is the beneficiary of a Preference Petition which is presently backlogged is ineligible for "adjustment". As an example, the priority date for the unskilled category under the third employment related preference is presently three and a half (3 1/2) years in arrears. Thus, a person who is in the United States and who has an approved employment third preference petition would be ineligible to file for Adjustment of Status until the priority date was current.

Second, the person must have been inspected and admitted or, alternatively, paroled into the United States. Proof of lawful admission into the United States will be the Form I-94 which was obtained by the foreign person at the border.

Third, the foreign person must not be otherwise excludable from the United States. Refer to the section entitled "General Exclusions" in this book for a list of these conditions.

Fourth, the foreign person must otherwise be deserving of the favorable exercise of discretion by the Immigration Officer. Even though Adjustment of Status is routinely granted where all of the other elements are present, it is still within the discretion of the Immigration Officer (or Judge) to deny the privilege of Adjustment of Status for good cause. Thus if a spouse of a United States citizen has gained entry into the United States by the fraudulent use of a B-2 visa and this fact is apparent, the Adjustment of Status application may be denied. This might occur if the couple while abroad realize that the foreign person will be denied immediate entry to the United States if they marry abroad, decide to have the foreign person enter the United States as a visitor and then immediately marry in the United States.

In addition to the above described discretionary right of refusal by the INS there are also certain statutorily (required by the law) ineligible classes of persons. They are as follows:

- alien crewmen (D - visa holders)

- aliens admitted as transients without visas, as for example someone who is travelling by airplane from Buenos Aires, Argentina to Toronto, Canada who is authorized to disembark at an intermediate U.S. airport.

- aliens who have violated the conditions of their present visa in any manner, as for example by engaging in unauthorized employment or by overstaying the authorized duration. There is an exception for immediate relatives of U.S. citizens. A spouse, for example, of a U.S. citizen is not prevented from filing for Adjustment of Status simply because he or she has violated the terms of his/her existing visa.

- aliens who enter into marriages with U.S. citizens after November, 1986 while they are in exclusion or deportation proceedings with the INS.

The privilege of Adjustment of Status may also be sought while a person is under exclusion or deportation hearings.

Adjustment of Status is essentially a procedural privilege. Denial of the application or ineligibility does not necessarily affect the substantive eligibility of a foreign person for permanent residency status. It does mean that the person will have to invest in an airplane ticket to the U.S. Consulate in his country of origin or in certain cases to a friendly U.S. Consulate in a third country in order to obtain his/her permanent visa.

2.13 - REFUGEES. This subsection deals with an immigration status which differs from all of the others described in this book. In order to take advantage of the benefits of the law with respect to either refugee or asylee designations the alien must establish certain proof which relates to political, ideological or sociological conditions in his home country which adversely and personally affect him. This proof involves issues which affect certain specific foreign policy interests of the United States and for these reasons this category has been treated separately in this book.

This area of law invites much litigation and discussion in the United States and is subject to changes in interpretation of law and in political direction depending upon world events. Certain political conditions may cause the United States to assume that a member of a particular group qualifies as a refugee while denying that status to other groups similarly situated.

The law defines a refugee as follows:

"(42) The term 'refugee' means (A) any person who is outside any country of such person's nationality or, in the case of a person having no nationality, is outside any country in which such person last habitually resided and who is unable or unwilling to return to, and is unable or unwilling to avail himself or herself of the protection of that country because of persecution or a well-founded fear of persecution on account of race, religion, nationality, membership in particular social group, or political opinion, or (B) in such special circumstances as the President after appropriate consultation (as defined in section 207 (e) of the Act) may specify, any person who is within the country of such person's nationality or, in the case of a person having no nationality within the country in which such person is habitually residing, and who is persecuted or who has a sell-founded fear of persecution on account of race, religion, nationality, membership in a particular social group, or political opinion. The term 'refugee' does not include any person who ordered, incited, assisted, or otherwise participated in the persecution of any person on account of race, religion, nationality, membership in particular social group, or political opinion."

One of the purposes of the above law was to adopt the major provisions of the UNITED NATIONS PROTOCOL RELATING TO THE STATUS OF REFUGEES to which the United States is a signatory. Also, the law attempts to establish a permanent and consistent method of admitting refugees and asylees to the United States. The following sections discuss and explain the principal features of the law.

2.13.a. - NUMERICAL LIMITATIONS. The law provides for a separate system of numerical limitations for refugees than that which is applicable to persons seeking permanent residence in the United States under the Preference System described in this book.

The refugee section of the immigration law establishes a mechanism by which the President of the United States with the advice and consent of the Congress establishes the total number of refugees which will be admitted in a given year as well as the numerical limit applicable to individual countries or sections of the world. The law provides for the exercise of executive discretion in the designation of those countries or sections of the world and thus the availability of refugee admissions may vary from year to year. The vagaries of U.S. foreign policy and the political conditions in other parts of the world may very well influence the President's decision as to the implementation of the refugee program in any given year.

2.13.b. - INDIVIDUAL ELIGIBILITY. A refugee as defined by the law is a person who is physically outside the United States. If a person is physically within or at the borders of the United States then he will be considered an applicant for asylum and thus will be subject to the eligibility requirements of that status as discussed in the following chapter.

The key provision in the refugee section as to eligibility is the requirement that the person be unwilling or unable to return to his home or other country because of persecution or a well-founded fear of persecution on account of race, religion, nationality, membership in a particular social group, or political opinion.

The law does not discriminate between western bloc or eastern bloc countries nor does it require that the person have actually fled from his home country. Obviously, persons who claim persecution by a country whose government or foreign policy is inimical to the United States have a much better chance of being adjudged refugees than persons who come from countries which are friendly to the United States. In order to prove that a person is subject to the conditions underlined above a person must prove first that the country is despotic and tyrannical and for that reason denies to the applicant the protection otherwise afforded to nationals of that country through the legal or political institutions of that country. Second, the person must prove that he himself will be the subject of persecution or that he has a well-founded fear of being persecuted.

The first requirement, proof as to the general despotic nature of the foreign regime, is easier to provide than the second requirement, proof of the persecution of the alien. Usually there will be more documentation available about the regime's behavior as to human rights and in certain instances the United States may already recognize the despotic nature of the foreign government. There are various documentary sources and human rights organizations which maintain information on the human rights environment in certain countries and these can be made available to an applicant for refugee status. The refugee applicant must prove that the home country's institutions and or policies are not available to protect persons like himself. The Department of State of the United States does not always agree with an applicant's assertion of the home country's despotic nature in which case the applicant has a heavy burden of persuasion. The second requirement as outlined above is very often the greatest impediment to a finding of refugee status when it is asserted by an individual who is not a member of a group that has been recognized as such by the Department of State. The applicant must present documented evidence that (s)he, personally or as member of a group, will be subject to persecution. For obvious reasons, the Immigration and Naturalization Service will not accept the mere self serving statement of the individual that (s)he is subject to persecution. Unless the individual is a member of a group of persons whom the United States government accepts as a persecuted group in a foreign country, the individual must provide documentary proof as to his personal exposure. As a matter of experience this requirement presents a greater burden to an applicant for asylum since by definition that person is already outside of the home country, probably within the national borders of the Untied States, and thus finds it difficult, if not impossible to obtain and present the type of documentary proof which the INS requires.

In addition to the above two requirements as to eligibility, the alien applicant also must be innocent of any acts of persecution, and must otherwise be a person of good moral character.

2.13.c - THE APPLICATION PROCESS. The applicant has the burden of proving that (s)he is eligible to be accorded the designation of refugee. The application itself is completed by the filing of Form I-590, biographic information on a Form G-325 and a fingerprint card for each person over the age of fourteen. In the event of a successful refugee application the spouse and children accompanying or coming to join the principal alien are entitled to derivative refugee status unless they have engaged in acts of persecution themselves.

The application process is conducted abroad either by the Immigration and Naturalization Service in those countries where it maintains offices or at certain designated U.S. consular posts abroad. In every case the applicant is subject to customary investigation for security and police purposes and is required to present a series of personal documents for verification. In addition the applicant is subject to medical examination to rule out certain communicative diseases.

If the application is approved, the refugee is authorized to enter the United States and is authorized to work and otherwise receive remuneration. After a period of one year has elapsed from the date of entry the alien is permitted to file an application for adjustment of status to that of a permanent resident alien. Before an alien may enter the

United States there must be proof that (s)he has been sponsored for employment and for a residence in the United States and that (s)he will not become a public charge. It is for this purpose that many volunteer and philanthropic agencies become active in the resettlement of aliens, even though the same purpose may be achieved by an individual, as is so often the case with respect to relatives or other members of a closely knit religious or ethnic group.

If an alien has been firmly settled in another country then he is not eligible for refugee status to the United States. The criteria for being firmly settled depends upon many factors such as the type of legal status the person has been granted as well as the nature of any restrictions that may have been imposed upon him which may limit the alien's ability to adapt reasonably to the new country.

ASYLUM

2.14 - ASYLUM. The law provides as follows with respect to asylum:

"Sec. 208(a) The Attorney General shall establish a procedure for an alien physically present in the United States or at a land border or port of entry, irrespective of such alien's status, to apply for asylum, and the alien may be granted asylum in the discretion of the Attorney General if the Attorney General determines that such alien is a refugee within the meaning of section 101 (a) (42) (A)."

"(b) Asylum granted under subsection (a) may be terminated if the Attorney General, pursuant to such regulations as the Attorney General may prescribe, determines that the alien is no longer a refugee within the meaning of the section 101(a) (42) (A) owing to a change in circumstances in the alien's country of nationality or, in the case of an alien's having no nationality, in the country in which the alien last habitually resided."

"(c) A spouse or child (as defined in section 101 (b) (1) (A), (B), (C), (D), or (E) of an alien who is granted asylum under subsection (a) may, if not otherwise eligible for asylum under such subsection, be granted the same status as the alien if accompanying, or following to join, such alien."

The principal difference between the Asylum and Refugee categories is that the former applies to those aliens who are already in the United States while the latter applies to persons outside the United States. The law provides for a procedure by which an asylee who has been admitted into the United States may have his spouse and/or child(ren) join him in the United States upon proof of the familial relationship.

The grant of Asylum status is discretionary. The Attorney General acting through his representatives in the Department of Immigration and Naturalization may withhold the granting of asylum for good cause. Thus, if an alien were to secrete himself into the United States and bypass the normal refugee process which was otherwise open to him, the grant of asylum could be denied on that basis.

Certain requests for asylum which are or may be politically sensitive are brought to the attention of the Department of State. These generally involve an asylum request from a national of a communist country and/or a diplomatic or consular officer of a foreign country. Requests for asylum are often made in deportation hearings as an alternative to deportation (Withholding of Deportation). The law mandates that an alien cannot be deported to a country where he will be subject to persecution for reasons and in a context that could categorize the alien as a refugee. While this remedy is mandatory, if the immigration judge determines the facts favorably to the alien's pleading, it is a very difficult remedy to obtain. The alien very rarely has the type of proof at hand to document that he, personally, would be the subject of persecution in the foreign land. There are various organizations in the United States that compile proof about the human rights violations of countries and these may be helpful in a particular case. The organization entitled AMNESTY INTERNATIONAL, 705 G Street, S.E. Washington, D.C. 20003, would be an excellent starting point for anyone who believes he is or should be entitled to receive asylum from a particular nation.

———

SECTION III

TEMPORARY NON-IMMIGRANT VISAS

In this section we shall discuss the most important and common non-immigrant visas. Since, except for the H-1B visa, there is no annual numerical limitation or quota on the number of non-immigrant visas that may be issued (except for H-1B visas), many more non-immigrant than immigrant visas are issued and utilized.

After a foreign person is inspected at the border and then admitted into the United States he is issued a small white card or piece of paper known as a Form I-94, which is the official entry document which establishes that the alien has been inspected at the border. This form documents that the person has lawfully entered the United States and also establishes the visa category in which he has been admitted as well as the designated duration of stay. This form should be carried by the foreign person at all times on his person in his passport. The length of time that the foreign person may remain in the United States is designated in the Form I-94 and not by the terminology of the visa which is stamped in the passport. Thus the legend on the B-1/B-2 visa which states that the bearer is entitled to unlimited entries to the United States does not mean that the person may remain in the United States for an indefinite period of time. It means that the person does not need to re-apply for another visa. The duration of time that he may remain in the United States is limited to the date indicated in the Form I-94.

There are several characteristics of non-immigrant visas that set them apart from the immigrant visas that were discussed in the previous chapters.

First, the non-immigrant visa grants the foreign person the privilege of entering the United States for only a temporary and defined period of time. This of course requires that the alien's intention as to his intended duration of stay must also be temporary.

Second, each particular visa imposes certain restrictions and conditions on the activities that the alien may engage in while he is in the United States. In other words, there are different visas for different activities to be conducted in the U.S. Thus, the tourist or visitor visa does not authorize employment, the student visa authorizes study at only a certain institution, the treaty investor visa authorizes employment only in a defined enterprise, and so forth.

There are many types of non-immigrant visas which will not be discussed in this book because they pertain to a very limited class of persons and are very specialized in their application. Examples of these visas are the NATO visa for NATO officials, the A-1 visa for diplomatic personnel and the I visa for news media reporters and representatives.

Very often a non-immigrant visa is more aptly suited to the needs of a foreign person than the immigrant visa, especially for investors, business persons and professionals. Furthermore, the non-immigrant visa can be obtained quickly, at least as compared to an immigrant visa. Since most non-immigrant visas are much more readily obtainable than immigrant visas, many foreign persons attempt to use the non-immigrant visa as a substitute for the immigrant visa. For all of the above factors there has been an increase in the demand for the non-immigrant visa as well as an increased scrutiny of non-immigrant petitions by the U.S. immigration authorities. Therefore, a thorough understanding of the limits, conditions and purposes of the various non-immigrant visas to the U.S.A. is essential to proper planning by the foreign person or entity. I cannot over-emphasize the importance of advanced and thorough planning by the foreign person. It may very well mean the difference between denial or approval of the visa petition.

<u>3.1 - THE B-1/B-2 VISA</u>. The B-visa is by far the most prevalent visa issued by the United States consular authorities for entry to the United States. For most foreign persons this is the easiest of all the non-immigrant visas to obtain. The B-1 visa is used for the conduct of specific categories of business in the United States, while the B-2 visa is issued to tourists or visitors for pleasure. In neither case, however, may the holder of the visa engage in activities which will result in compensation such as wages, tips, fees, commissions, etc., and the "business" contemplated by the B-1 visa does not include the active management of a business or commercial enterprise in the United States. A B-1 visa holder may properly attend business meetings, court hearings, etc., and may engage in professional or commercial undertakings so long as any compensation is earned and paid from abroad, while the B-2 visa holders, as already indicated, are limited to non-business, visitor activities.

The B-1/B-2 visa is obtained at a U.S. consular post abroad and is valid for an initial entry of up to six months. This period may be extended for good cause for an additional period of six months but extensions beyond that are very difficult to obtain. Occasionally I am asked by foreign visitors if these time limitations can be legally circumvented by merely taking short trips out of the United States shortly before the expiration of stay which is listed in the I-94. My answer is that the border inspection officer has the right to deny entry to an individual if the border officer is convinced that the person is actually living in the United States permanently. In colloquial terms I invite the questioner to assume that the border inspection officer is just as astute as the foreign person. Thus, the officer is able to deduce that someone who has spent the majority of time (perhaps, the last sixteen months) over a lengthy period (perhaps the last eighteen months or so) of time in the United States is probably in fact an immigrant-without a proper visa--and is therefore excludable.

In order to qualify for the B-1/B-2 visa the foreign person must hold a valid passport or other travel document from his home country and must establish to the satisfaction of the U.S. visa officer the following:

1. He has a permanent domicile outside of the United States which he has no intention of abandoning.

2. He has the necessary financial capacity to conduct his business or pleasure trip in the United States and has a round trip ticket from the transportation carrier.

3. He is not otherwise disqualified (excludable) from entering the United States for reasons such as having a criminal record, etc.

While the legal requirements are fairly simple to meet, persons from developing countries may find it difficult to obtain this visa if they are unable to prove that they have enough motivation to depart the United States within the time period established by the immigration officer at the border. The Consular visa officers very often use "profiles" to determine whether a person might be a poor risk for receiving a B-1/B-2 visa. For example, a young, unmarried person without a job or other visible means of support would probably be denied a B-1/B-2 visa because there would be insufficient motivation for that person to return to the country of origin. The situation would be worsened if the young person also has close relatives in the United States and comes from an underdeveloped country. In a situation in which one or more of the above factors is present, I recommend that the visa applicant prepare for the Consular officer's inquiry by organizing <u>documentary</u> proof that he/she has strong motivation to depart the United States at the conclusion of the visit. This might entail proof of a good job in the home country, the ownership of valuable property, as well as the existence of other strong economic, emotional and cultural ties to the home country. Remember, the presumption is that the visa applicant is not entitled to the visa until he proves otherwise to the satisfaction of the consular visa officer.

The IMMIGRATION REFORM AND CONTROL ACT OF 1986 established a visa waiver pilot program which provides that aliens from designated countries can enter the United States as visitors for a period of up to three (3) months without a visa. The program was initially limited to visitors from the United Kingdom. Visitors from the United Kingdom are considered to be persons who have the right of permanent abode there and are unrestricted in their travel within the United Kingdom. The Visa Waiver Pilot program now includes the following countries:

Italy	France	Japan
Sweden	Switzerland	The Netherlands
Germany	Spain	United Kingdom
Austria	New Zealand	Finland
Belgium	Denmark	Norway
Iceland	Luxembourg	San Marino
Andorra	Monaco	Liechtenstein

Visitors from the above countries who enter on the basis of the Visa Waiver program are subject to certain restrictions, such as the inability to extend their stay, change their non-immigrant status or adjust to permanent residence. The visitor may still be barred from entering the United States at the border if he cannot, for any reason, substantiate that he seeks to enter the United States as a visitor. As of the writing of this book, there has been insufficient experience with this program to state any trends under this program. Under all circumstances, anyone entering the United States, even under this visa waiver pilot program, should be able to substantiate and support all the requirements for entrance under the B-visa.

I do not recommend that a prospective business investor or executive utilize this program for preparatory or research visits to the United States unless he/she is certain that he will not need to extend his visit or that he will not be required to change his status to the visa category sought. This is because of the inflexibility of the program which prohibits extensions of stay or change of status.

3.2 TREATY TRADER/INVESTOR (E-1, E-2). This is one of the most important non-immigrant visas. The United States has signed treaties of navigation and commerce with certain other nations which provide among other things that nationals of those countries may enter and work in the United States under certain defined conditions. If the treaty trader, or treaty investor is a company then the employee in the United States must have the same nationality as the company. The employee must usually perform managerial or executive functions, although if the employee possesses some specialized skill not otherwise obtainable in the United States, then a purely staff or labor position could support the E visa. The visa authorizes an initial duration of stay of up to two years and there is no limit on the total time that the employee may remain in the United States with proper extensions, provided he continues in the employment which originally supported the visa. The E visa holder's spouse and minor dependents are also accorded the same visa. Another advantage of the E visa is that it is unnecessary to establish that the visa holder continues to maintain a home in the foreign country to which he intends to return.

The two types of activities and their corresponding visas that are contemplated are as follows:

3.2.a. - THE E-1 VISA: This visa is known as the treaty <u>trader</u> visa and benefits nationals of the treaty partner who are engaged in a "substantial" volume of trade with the United States. While it is not possible to define precisely what the term "substantial" means, it requires a volume of trade that is sufficient to at least support the employee in the United States. The trade transactions do not have to be individually large as long as they are numerous and the total percentage volume of trade must be at least 51% by and between the United States and the treaty country.

As of January 1, 1989, the Immigration & Naturalization Service agreed to extend the term "trade" to include "the exchange, purchase, or sale of goods and/or services". Goods are tangible commodities of merchandise having intrinsic value, excluding money, securities and negotiable instruments. Services are economic activities whose outputs are other than tangible goods. Such activities include, but are not limited to, banking, insurance, transportation, communications and data processing, advertising, accounting, design and engineering, management consulting, and tourism. This new definition greatly expands the applicability of the treaty/trader provisions since it now accepts the modern reality that much of international trade has to do with the movement of services rather than goods and commodities.

The countries that have <u>E-1</u> treaty privileges are as follows:

Argentina	Austria	Belgium
Bolivia	Brunei(Borneo)	China
Colombia	Costa Rica	Denmark
Estonia	Ethiopia	Finland
France	Germany	Greece
Honduras	Iran	Ireland
Israel	Italy	Japan
Korea	Latvia	Liberia
Luxembourg	The Netherlands	Nicaragua
Norway	Pakistan	Paraguay
The Philippines	Spain	Sultanate of Muscat and Oman
Switzerland	Thailand	Togo
United Kingdom of Great Britain		Vietnam
Yugoslavia		

3.2.b. - THE E-2 VISA. This visa is known as the treaty <u>investor</u> visa and authorizes an alien who is a national of a treaty country to enter the United States for an extended period of time to invest and develop an entrepreneurial venture.

ELIGIBILITY: The investment must be of a "substantial" nature and must not be marginal. The law does not establish a minimum amount of capital required to fulfill the requirement of "substantial", nor is the term "substantial" defined clearly, nor is there a mathematical formula that can be used to discover this meaning. In addition, the term "substantial" is subject to varying interpretation in different consular posts, and perhaps different consular officers in the same post.

With respect to the start up of a new enterprise which is being developed by the investor, substantial is very often determined by a comparison of the size of other similar types of businesses. The investor is usually more clearly at risk in these start up enterprises than would be the case where the investor is purchasing an existing business. In addition to the overall size of the business, the number of employees contemplated is also very important in predicting the success of the application. The more employees are employed the less emphasis there will be on the question of whether or not the investment is substantial. In start up enterprises, there is usually less of a problem in establishing to the satisfaction of the U.S. consul that the investment is committed, as a precondition to the issuance of the visa. Since there was no pre-existing business structure in place, prior to the foreign person's investments, it is not logical to expect the business to function before the visa is actually issued to the alien.

Original "start up" ventures, however, are fraught with risk from a purely business standpoint and most business consultants would agree that, all else being equal, it is preferable to purchase an existing, ongoing business or commercial enterprise. The United States has a relatively free economy which, while providing the freedom to succeed, also provides the environment to fail. The statistics kept by the Small Business Administration of the U.S. Department of Commerce indicate that the majority of new enterprises fail within the first two (2) years of existence. One can only deduce that for a foreign person who does not have very much insight into the norms and customs of the commercial community into which he/she ventures, the risk of failure is at least as high as it is for U.S. residents. I cannot prove it but I suspect that the percentage of failure by foreign investors with respect to "start up" enterprises is higher than it is for U.S. residents.

As a result, many foreign persons would rather invest in an enterprise that is already in existence and is already functioning. Enter the world of immigration. The rules and regulations require that a foreign person invest a relatively high percentage of the price of the business opportunity -- indeed, much higher than is required by sellers of U.S. resident purchasers. My "rule of thumb" for determining what is substantial with respect to the purchase of an existing business is that the investor should purchase the largest business possible with a direct investment of at least 50% of the price of the business.

Substantiality is very often determined by the use of a "proportionality" or "relative" test. The proportionality test is used in analyzing the acquisition by a foreign person of an existing enterprise. Pursuant to IMMACT90, the Department of State has issued rules and regulations which require that for the purchase of existing business enterprises where the purchase price is $500,000.00 or less, the investor must invest up to 75% of the value of the business. For investments greater than $500,000.00 and up to $1,000,000.00 the foreign person must invest at least 50% of the purchase price of the business. In my home state of Florida, businesses are usually purchased with considerably less capital than the amounts required by these regulations. Thus, a foreign person who purchases a business strictly in accordance with these regulations may be immediately placed at a competitive disadvantage unless he/she also has sufficient additional capital for operating expenses and other business contingencies. The regulations obviously were not written by persons with practical business knowledge. An immigration attorney colleague satirically remarked to me that any person who applies for an E-2 visa in strict accordance with the above proportionality guidelines should be rejected for having a lack of entrepreneurial ability.

The above proportionality tests are not mandatory and may be modified in individual cases but I fear that the bureaucratic tendency is to use these guidelines as "white line" tests, and when a particular investment does not fall within the proportions outlined, there will be a presumption of ineligibility. This is especially unfortunate since often the foreign person may be very experienced and knowledgeable in business while the examining consular officer who has the authority to issue or deny the visa may be lacking in business experience and acumen.

One technique that may avoid the economic problem in the proportionality test is to divide the transaction so that the capital of the foreign person in the correct proportion purchases the substantial or key assets or components of the business and the other assets would be purchased in a related though separate transaction. There are many variations of this technique that may be applicable in particular circumstances and it is imperative that proper planning be conducted prior to the execution of any documents for the acquisition of the business enterprise. A competent immigration attorney and competent business consultant are essential in this type of situation.

Of course, in the investment of a large sum of money such as would be the case of cash or property in the amount of $1,000,000.00 or more, "substantiality" may be assumed as a result of its sheer size, even though it may not approximate the recommended percentages. In most instances, the concept of "substantiality" is dependent on the type of business that is being developed as well as the proportion of equity invested by the alien. The investment cannot be "marginal" and very often the concepts of "substantial" and "marginal" are interrelated. The concept of "marginality" will be explained in greater detail further on in this chapter. The following is an example of the "substantiality" concept.

An investment in a heavy marine construction firm would require millions of dollars, since barges, cranes, tug boats, and other such ancillary equipment is costly. Compare this type of investment with an investment in a wholesale distribution business for which the only capital investment required other than the wholesale inventory would be warehouse space, office furniture, perhaps the purchase of certain intangible assets, such as contract rights, etc. This business could be sufficiently capitalized with, let us say, $75,000.00. In the second business, it is very likely that the Immigration and Naturalization Service or the U.S. consul abroad will require an investment of at least fifty percent of the total amount required for the business, whereas for the first company a lesser percentage is probably acceptable, if the investment were large and if the investor was still directing the enterprise.

INVESTOR'S OWN FUNDS. The U.S. consul abroad will usually require documentary proof that the funds invested are the investor's own. Any person interested in this visa should begin to gather up all the documentation to trace the funds from his account in the home country into the United States. The U.S. consul will want documentary proof as to the origin and/or ownership of the funds and will usually not settle for anything less than this. This may be a problem for certain investors who live in countries where there is a restriction on the conversion of local funds into foreign currency, or that may have various restrictions on the expatriation of capital. It is not uncommon for persons of means in these countries to have moved certain amounts of their funds to a third country and to have used various legal and accounting maneuvers to isolate these funds from themselves. Thus, it may be imprudent for that person to reveal that he is the actual owner of funds which he now seeks to move into the United States. Even though this may be a common practice in a particular country, the U.S. consul will still require documentary proof that funds brought into the United States belong to the investor. Where an individual secretes large amounts of cash out of his country, appears at the U.S. border and files the appropriate customs declarations with respect to the funds that he is bringing into the United States, the U.S. consul or Immigration and Naturalization Service under the E-2 requirements may still require the foreign investor prove the cash funds he brought with him and declared at the U.S. border are in fact his funds.

While the rules and regulations require the foreign investor to utilize his own funds, loans that are guaranteed by the personal credit of the investor will suffice to meet the standard of "substantiality." Loan proceeds that are collateralized by the assets that are being acquired by the foreign investor do not count as part of the investment for E-2 visa purposes. If the investor buys or establishes a business on a heavily leveraged basis, with very little personal financial risk, then the investment will fail for purposes of the visa petition.

The investor is not required to invest only cash into the enterprise. Equipment, fixtures, inventory and other valuable tangible assets are also valid assets for investment. Even intangibles such as patent rights or royalty or other contract rights can be used in the valuation of the alien's investments as long as they can be objectively appraised.

INVESTOR TO DIRECT AND MANAGE. It is imperative that the alien prove he is entering the United States to direct and manage the investment/enterprise. This requirement is dependent upon proof that the investor owns and/or controls the enterprise that is the subject of the visa application. While ordinarily the alien must establish that he owns at least 50% of the equity in the enterprise, it may be possible to demonstrate control by contracts or other agreements that essentially place the management and control of the enterprise in the hands of the alien.

Logic alone would indicate that if the alien is not in control of the investment and does not need to be present in the United States in order to manage it, the visa would be unnecessary.

ACTIVE ENTERPRISE. The rules and regulations also require that the investment be an active enterprise as opposed to a passive investment. Investments in vacant land or in stocks, bonds, mutual funds, etc., will not qualify the investor for an E-2 visa, regardless of the amount involved. The E-2 visa was created to bring into the United States key individuals whose presence is required to make an enterprise grow. Obviously, if the investment is one which does not require the personal involvement of the investor, the E-2 visa would not be appropriate for that person. This is, of course, a generality, and there may be some rare exceptions. There may also be some cases which will require close analysis if the line between passive and active is not clear. An example is someone who invests in the business of land or home development. While the ownership of land per se is insufficient as an entrepreneurial investment, someone who assumes the active entrepreneurial risk of developing land for commercial purposes would be an investor for E-2 purposes.

The points discussed above may be difficult to rationalize in certain cases. I remember specifically a situation some years ago when a prominent real estate broker brought to my office two wealthy European investors. These gentlemen were about to purchase through her a large tract of orange groves, already under lease to an orange grove operator. The investors would not be involved at all in the orange grove business and sought to make their profit by re-selling the grove in the future. The foreign individuals were about to invest more than a million dollars, U.S. cash, for the property, since it provided a favorable rate of return and was fairly secure. The real estate professional stood to earn a sizeable commission on the sale. The investors, however, had one condition on their investment, and that was that they obtain an E visa, so they could enter the U.S. and spend extended periods of time here at will. After analyzing the investment and their participation in the investment, I came to the conclusion that the investment would clearly not qualify for the E-2 visa and I so informed everyone. The investors were disappointed that the large investment that they were willing to make would not entitle them to the visa, but were happy to find this out prior to making the commitment to complete the transaction. The real estate agent wrung her hands in despair as she witnessed the demise of her commission. However, it was not possible to obtain an E-2 visa for the prospective foreign investors under the circumstances of that investment, and as they had structured it. Had they purchased the investment on the understanding that they would qualify for this visa, they would have been disappointed later, and they would not have thought highly of the real estate professional who sold them the property.

MARGINALITY. The projected return on investment must provide a rate of return or the possibility of return, which a prudent investor would ordinarily expect. Thus, if the investment would provide only sufficient funds for the person to make a living, the investment would fail for E-2 visa purposes. There is a requirement that the person have income from other sources and is not depending upon the business investment as his sole means of livelihood. In this regard, the foreign person will be asked to document the other income which will then be compared with the expected return on the U.S. investment. This is very often a difficult concept for the foreign person to grasp because it is a negative concept; that is, in order to be successful in his visa application the investor must prove that the proposed investment does not have the characteristic of "marginality".

Another element of the concept of marginality is whether or not the investment will provide employment for U.S. citizens and/or residents. If the proposed business investment will provide for employment of other persons, the less likely the investment will be found to be marginal. Thus, if the business will only support the investor and one or two other subsidiary employees, an investment may not support an E-2 visa, unless the other factors described are present in a substantial degree. If the nature of the business is such that large numbers of employees are not normally necessary, such as would be the case if the alien investor were a commercial artist, then the employment requirement can be relaxed. This is because the nature of the business or endeavor, ie., the creation of art, depends upon the unique and particular talent of the investor, which efforts cannot be delegated to other employees.

The more U.S. persons that will be employed by the business, the less attention or importance will be placed on the profitability of the business. The requirements described above are all interrelated and are somewhat interdependent.

Let us examine the following example:

A restaurant is offered for sale by a U.S. seller at a price of $175,000. The transaction requires a total cash investment of only $75,000, since the present U.S. owner is willing to finance the balance ($100,000.00) of the purchase price. Indeed, this is a debt to equity ratio that would be customary in many areas in the United States. Furthermore, let us assume in our hypothetical transaction that the alien investor reasonably expects to derive a salary of $25,000 per annum and does not have income from any other source with which to sustain himself. The INS and/or the Department of State (U.S. consulate abroad) will probably decide that a $75,000 investment is not in and of itself substantial under these circumstances. Secondly, they will decide that a $25,000 return, where there is no other income from any other sources indicates that the investment is one that will merely provide this person with a minimum salary. Thus, this investment will probably fail for lack of substantiality and for being marginal in nature. If, on the other hand, the investor could show that he was rehabilitating a troubled business and was therefore saving the jobs --better yet, if the foreign investor could show an increase in the number of employees, the investment might be approved, especially if the investor could show that the amount invested was more than the norm or more than what would normally be required to establish or purchase a similar restaurant in the area. One cannot over emphasize the importance of documentary evidence to establish the veracity and accuracy of all assertions concerning the concept of "substantial" investment and the concomitant lack of "marginality".

A general guideline, as of the date of this book, for the minimum amount of cash required to meet the test of substantiality is $100,000 U.S. In certain U.S. consulates abroad, $100,000 would be considered minimal, thus, this figure must be considered only as a rule of thumb and must be analyzed in light of the type of business, the investment, the rate of return, and all of the other factors described in this section. Nonetheless, on an overall basis, an investment of less than this sum would to most U.S. consuls be considered, insubstantial, per se. Of course, if the business enterprise involves a service business, then a relatively small amount of capital, say $50,000.00 might be considered substantial, especially where the investor possesses special and unique skills such as personal ability and talent as would be the case for an artist or architect. For example, in the case of an architect, engineer or other designer who purchases and installs state-of-the-art computers, software and printers containing advanced "computer aided design" (CAD) features, the office headquarters might not require much more than standard office furniture in order to be a complete and properly functioning enterprise.

The "proportionality" test does not apply if the foreign person develops or creates a new business. In this event, substantiality will be established by proof that the amount of capital invested in the creation of the new enterprise represents an amount which is considered substantial by other members of the industry. It may be necessary to conduct a survey of the industry in order to establish this fact. The investor should still invest at least 50% of the fair market value of the assets.

As stated previously, the Department of State and the INS are wary of purported investments that may be nothing more than an attempt to immigrate to the United States in circumvention of the normal immigrant visa process. Consequently, these authorities look for evidence of immigrant intent in non-immigrant visa applications. In the writer's judgment, the purchase by an investor of a home in the United States before the non-immigrant visa has been granted is a tactical error.

For instance, in the case of an E-2 visa applicant, the money invested in a private dwelling such as a house or condominium apartment, is basically wasted as concerns the amount of capital available to satisfy the substantiality requirement of the law. This is especially true when the proportion of cash investment in the home exceeds that in the business. It does seem in these instances that the "cart is before the horse". In my geographic area in particular, the lovely State of Florida, most prospective foreign investors with whom I speak are either planning to or have already acquired an expensive home, sometimes for cash. I generally advise my clients that unless they are sufficiently wealthy that the purchase of the home represents an insignificant economic undertaking, they should defer that purchase until their investment has firmly rooted. I have spoken to foreign persons who erroneously believed they met the substantiality requirement by investing $150,000.00 in a home as well as $50,000.00 in a business.

This is not a rigid rule, of course. In certain instances a home purchase at the inception of a business investment can be objectively justified--but I do not believe it prudent to impose that additional burden on the application. It is better to approach the situation conservatively and patiently by concentrating on the business first and the personal accommodations second. The law does not now require the alien to maintain a home abroad nor does it require specific evidence of the alien's intent to return to the country of origin. Nonetheless, it is an excellent technique, especially in marginal investment applications, to be able to demonstrate voluntarily that the alien does in fact maintain a foreign residence and that his/her interest in acquiring or developing the U.S. enterprise is purely financial.

The United States has signed treaties of friendship and commerce providing for E-2 treaty investor benefits with the following countries:

Argentina	Austria	Belgium
China	Colombia	Costa Rica
Ethiopia	France	Germany
Honduras	Iran	Italy
Japan	Korea	Liberia
Luxembourg	Netherlands	Norway
Oman	Pakistan	Paraguay
Philippines	Spain	Surinam
Switzerland	Thailand	Togo
United Kingdom	Vietnam	Yugoslavia
Australia	Sweden	

In addition, as a result of the ratification by the Canadian Parliament of the U.S.-Canada Free Trade Act on January 1, 1989, Canadians are now eligible to obtain the E visas.

Employees of E-Visa Traders or Investors. If the E-Visa applicant is not the Trader or Investor principal, then his job must be either managerial or executive in nature or he must be a highly trained or other specially qualified person and he must have the same nationality as the E-Treaty principal. The rules and regulations state that the employee must

"...be engaged in duties of a supervisory or executive character, or if he is or will be employed in a minor capacity, he must have specific qualifications that will make services essential to the efficient operation of the employer's enterprise and will not be employed solely in an unskilled, manual capacity."

IMMACT90 requires the Department of State and the Immigration and Naturalization Service to issue new regulations defining the details for issuance of the E-2 visa to employees of E-2 visa employers. As of this date, the final regulations have not been issued and there seems to be a difference of opinion between the above two agencies of government with respect to the degree to which the employer must demonstrate an inability to find and hire local employees as a prerequisite to hiring an alien under this visa category.

In a new enterprise, the rules on the essentiality are somewhat relaxed so long as proof is given that after the start up phase, the foreign employees will be replaced by U.S. personnel who will be trained to take over their jobs.

3.2.c. - ADVANTAGES OF THE E-VISA. The advantages of an E-2 visa for qualified persons are as follows:

The visa may be renewed indefinitely as long as the investment originally supporting the E-visa continues in existence, although the visa is initially granted for up to five years at most U.S. Consulates. The duration of the initial E visa is dependent upon the duration of similar visas extended to U.S. investors by the other signatory country. Also the E Visa investor does not need to maintain a foreign domicile to which he intends to return. Thus, the expense of maintaining two residences can be avoided. However, as a result of the attitude and working philosophy of the U.S. Consulate, I still recommend to my clients that they maintain a Canadian domicile as well as other close contacts with Canada in order to establish the temporary intent that is still required of an E visa applicant. Additionally, employment by family members is not normally viewed as a violation of status, even though the rules do not specifically sanction such employment. However, under the terms of the Immigration Reform and Control Act of 1986, it is doubtful whether a family member would be employable in the United States as employers now face criminal and civil sanctions for employing a person who is not otherwise authorized to work.

Another advantage of the E-visa is its flexibility. It does not require the foreign person to have acted in a particular business form in his home country. Unlike the situation with the L Visa, the individual by investing the funds, can qualify for the E-2 visa himself even if he has operated in the past and intends to operate in the future as a sole proprietor. Additionally, the investor does not need to prove that he is an executive or manager, etc., but merely prove that he is in a position to direct and manage the enterprise. This has been interpreted by rule and regulation and case law to mean that he must be in control of the enterprise. This distinction eliminates many of the technical problems involved in proving the status of executive or manager as indicated previously.

Procedure. The visa processing should normally occur at the U.S. consulate abroad. The E-2 visa is particularly subject to attack on the basis of "preconceived intent" if an application is made in the U.S. for a change of status from some other non-immigrant visa.

There is no special form that is used to initiate an E-visa application. Some U.S. consulates have a questionnaire which they have formulated while others operate more informally. In any event, the consul will require proof of all the elements outlined in this chapter so an individual applying for an E-visa should have all of the requirements documented. Even though not required, it is strongly recommended that an individual applying for this visa, as well as certain other temporary visas, utilize the services of an experienced immigration professional to assist him in marshalling the proofs required and to answer any of the questions of the U.S. consul. There is a saying that there is no second chance to make a favorable first impression and it would be imprudent to submit an E-1/E-2 visa application that did not evidence care and consideration. In many cases, a consul will appreciate having a professional handling the application because many problems can be avoided.

There is another variation of the intent problem which has already been discussed in previous chapters which may affect holders of non-immigrant visas. Since it is often easier to obtain one particular visa as opposed to another (for example, the B-2 visitor visa) an alien might be tempted to enter the United States on one visa and then after he is in the United States, file an application for a change to a different visa. There is nothing wrong with this procedure, if the change of intent is genuine. If the immigration authorities believe that the alien entered the United States with a preconceived intent to apply for a change of visa arrival, then the requested visa may be denied just for that reason.

3.2.d. - BILATERAL INVESTMENT TREATIES. Shortly before the publication of this book, the United States Senate ratified a series of bilateral accords known as BILATERAL INVESTMENT TREATIES (BIT) with the following countries:

Bangladesh	Cameroon	Egypt
Grenada	Morocco	Senegal
Turkey	Zaire	

The accords with Bangladesh, Morocco and Turkey have not yet been ratified by those countries and there are pending BIT accords with Haiti and Panama. The advantage of these BIT's is that a company or person who is a citizen of those countries may obtain an E-visa for an executive or managerial person who is a citizen of a country other than the BIT country involved. Thus, as an example, if an Egyptian company or businessman wishes to invest in the United States and needs to employ a manager or executive, he may choose to hire an employee from a country other than Egypt and that person will be accorded an E visa. Please compare this with the requirements that otherwise apply to the E provisions of the treaties of trade and commerce which the United States has signed with other countries, as described in this chapter. In those agreements, an employee of the E-1 or E-2 entity must also be a citizen of the same treaty country.

3.3 - CANADA AND CANADIANS: SPECIAL ADVANTAGES.

Canada has traditionally been treated in a special and generally preferred manner by the immigration system of the United States. Canadians (together with certain classes of Mexican citizens) have not needed visas to enter the United States. This, of course, did not mean that the immigration law did not apply to Canadians, rather that Canadians entering the United States merely had to demonstrate to the officer at the border that they were otherwise qualified to enter in whatever visa category applied. Furthermore, since Canada does not have a treaty of navigation and commerce with the United States, its citizens did not have the advantages of the E visas.

On January 2, 1988, the President of the United States and the Prime Minister of Canada signed a bilateral accord known as the Free Trade Agreement (FTA). This agreement entered into effect on January 1, 1989 upon ratification by the Canadian Parliament. This agreement addresses topics such as trade, commerce, and tariffs, but in order to facilitate the overall trade purposes of the act, also made some major sweeping changes in the immigration procedures of both countries. The immigration provisions do not replace the substantive immigration law, but rather modify the existing law. The immigration provisions of the FTA present very favorable changes to the Canadian business person/investor.

For example, the legislation and administration Rules and Regulations make the Treaty/Trader Investor visa classification available to Canadian citizens for the first time. All of the provisions and requirements as described in this book, that apply to E Treaty applicants, now apply to Canadian citizens. Canadian citizens applying for E visas in the Western Hemisphere do not need to possess a passport and may have their visa issued on a separate document (Form OF-232).

The provisions of the FTA apply only to Canadian citizens. "Landed immigrants" of Canada are not benefitted. In order to qualify under the appropriate division of the FTA, an individual must fit within the prerequisite definition of "business person" who is engaged in the trade of goods or services or investment activities; and "temporary entry" is defined as "entry without the intent to establish permanent residence". With respect to the latter requirement, all of the previous discussion on intention applies.

There are four groups of non-immigrants covered by the FTA. They are as follows:

1. Business visitors

a) Business visitors may come temporarily to the United States for research and design, growth, manufacture and production, marketing, sales, distribution, after sales service and general service. An alien who qualifies under this provision is not entitled to receive salary or remuneration from a United States source. However, a business visitor may receive incidental expenses from a United States source.

b) The initial entry period is for one year and the rules state that the extension may be granted in six month increments. At the date of the publication of this book, the limit of the duration of stay under this category was unclear, but it would seem there is no precise limitation as to how many extensions may be granted even after the original one year admission. This may change over time as rules and regulations are added by the

Immigration and Naturalization Service. Of course, accompanying family members, that is the spouse or children of a Canadian citizen, may be admitted under the same terms and conditions of the principal.

2. Canadian Citizen Traders and Investors

a) As stated previously, until the passage of the FTA, Canada had not been covered by friendship and commerce treaty, so the E visa provisions were unavailable to Canadian citizens. The FTA extends the benefits of the E Treaty Trader provisions to Canadian citizens.

b) A Canadian citizen seeking admission under this section must apply for a visa from a U.S. Consular Officer abroad in order to enter under E visa status. Regulations as to the issuance of these visas will be published shortly by the Department of State. Please also note that services have now been added to the above definition of "Trade".

3. Intra-Company Transferees

a) The only substantial change in the application of the L-1 visa provisions to Canadian citizens is that the citizen may have the option of presenting all of his supporting documents, etc. at the designated border points, thus circumventing the need for previously approved petitions by the Immigration and Naturalization Service. This, I believe, will be difficult to implement as the volume of documentation required for these visas can sometimes be quite onerous and unless one arrives at the border point early (three hours is recommended), it is doubtful that the border official will be able to properly analyze the documents. Unless the INS border inspector has sufficient time to review the alien's documents, the foreign person will be admitted under parole and an appointment will be scheduled at the Immigration and Naturalization office nearest the Canadian citizen's intended place of work in order to have the supporting documents thoroughly reviewed.

4. Canadian Citizens Seeking Classification in Activities at a Professional level.

a) Under the provisions of the FTA, Canadian citizens can enter the United States temporarily to "engage in business activities at a professional level". In order to qualify under this category, the individual must provide proof of Canadian citizenship and documentation showing that he is engaged in one of the professions listed in Schedule Two to Annex 1502.1. This " Schedule 2" is attached at the end of this subsection. An important advantage of this provision is that the Canadian citizen will be able to enter the United States without first having had a petition filed by an employer requesting the alien's admission. The implementing legislation of the FTA amends the Immigration and Naturalization Act and includes as professionals Disaster Relief and Insurance Claims Adjusters, Computer Systems Analysts and Management Consultants. The H-1 regulations have required in the past that an individual possess a baccalaureate or other advanced degree to qualify as a professional. The FTA provides an individual lacking one of these degrees must demonstrate at least four years of experience, or the equivalent of the time normally spent acquiring a baccalaureate degree in the United States.

Although the FTA does not require that a petition be filed on behalf of the business professional, the implementing regulation specifies that the level of documentation "be on a par with that required for non-immigrant classifications for which petitions are required." Documentation which must be presented include the following:

1. The professional activity to be engaged in;

2. The purpose of entry;

3. The anticipated length of stay;

4. The educational qualifications or appropriate credentials which demonstrate that the Canadian citizen has professional level status;

5. Proof that the Canadian citizen complies with all applicable state laws and licensing requirements for the occupation to be engaged in;

6. The arrangements for remuneration for services to be rendered.

7. Extensions of stay may be granted in increments of one year. The application is to be accompanied by a letter from the employer confirming the continuing need for the alien's temporary services and specifying the additional time needed.

b) Duration - A Canadian citizen who otherwise qualifies, will be provided with an I-94 Form under the classification symbol TC with an initial entry period not to exceed one year.

In addition to the above, Section 214(e) provides for the admission to the United States of Canadian citizens who are coming to engage in professional activities, as defined by the FTA. A list of those specific professions which have been identified by the act and enabling legislation is as follows:

<u>LIST 2</u>

- Accountant - baccalaureate degree

- Architect - baccalaureate degree or provincial license

- Computer Systems Analyst - baccalaureate degree

- Disaster relief claims adjuster - baccalaureate degree or three years experience in the field of claims adjustment

- Economist - baccalaureate degree

- Engineer - baccalaureate degree or provincial license

- Forester - baccalaureate degree or provincial license

- Graphic Designer - baccalaureate degree, or post secondary diploma and three years experience

- Hotel Manager - baccalaureate degree and 3 years experience

- Land Surveyor - baccalaureate degree or provincial/Federal license

- Lawyer - member of bar in province, L.L.B., J.D., L.L.L., or B.C.L.

- Librarian - M.L.S. or B.L.S.

- Management Consultant - baccalaureate degree or five years experience in consulting or related field

- Mathematician - baccalaureate degree

- Medical/Allied Professionals

    - Clinical lab technologist - baccalaureate degree
    - Dentist - D.D.S., D.M.D., or provincial license
    - Dietician - baccalaureate degree or provincial license
    - Medical technologist - baccalaureate degree
    - Nutritionist - baccalaureate degree
    - Occupational therapist - baccalaureate degree or provincial license
    - Pharmacist - baccalaureate degree or provincial license
    - Physician - (teaching and/or research only) M.D., or provincial license
    - Physio/Physical therapist - baccalaureate degree or provincial license
    - Psychologist - provincial license
    - Recreational therapist - baccalaureate degree

- Registered Nurse - Provincial license

- Veterinarian - D.V.M., D.M.V. or provincial license

- Range Manager (Range Conservationist) - baccalaureate degree

- Research Assistant (Working in a Post Secondary Educational Institution) - baccalaureate degree

- Scientific technician/technologist - must work in direct support of professionals in the following disciplines: Chemistry, geology, geophysics, meteorology, physics, astronomy, agricultural sciences, biology, or forestry - must possess theoretical knowledge of the discipline; - must solve practical problems in the discipline--must apply principles of the discipline to basic or applied research

- Scientist

    - Agriculturist (Agronomist) - baccalaureate degree
    - Animal breeder - baccalaureate degree
    - Animal scientist - baccalaureate degree
    - Apiculturist - baccalaureate degree
    - Astronomer - baccalaureate degree
    - Biochemist - baccalaureate degree
    - Biologist - baccalaureate degree
    - Chemist - baccalaureate degree
    - Dairy Scientist - baccalaureate degree
    - Entomologist - baccalaureate degree
    - Epidemiologist - baccalaureate degree
    - Geneticist - baccalaureate degree
    - Geologist - baccalaureate degree
    - Geophysicist - baccalaureate degree
    - Horticulturist - baccalaureate degree
    - Meteorologist - baccalaureate degree
    - Pharmacologist - baccalaureate degree
    - Physicist - baccalaureate degree
    - Plant Breeder - baccalaureate degree

- Poultry Scientist - baccalaureate degree
- Soil Scientist - baccalaureate degree
- Sylviculturist (forestry specialist) - baccalaureate degree
- Teacher
  - College - baccalaureate degree
  - Seminary - baccalaureate degree
  - University - baccalaureate degree

- Technical Publications writer - baccalaureate degree, or post secondary diploma and three (3) years experience

- Urban Planner - baccalaureate degree

- Vocational counselor - baccalaureate degree

The Canadian citizen must present the Immigration & Naturalization inspector at the port of entry an adjudication verification of citizenship, a letter and any other required documents which demonstrate that the individual possesses the requisite educational background and experience for the profession claimed. He must also establish that he is qualified to engage in the employment indicated. Of course, a dependent spouse and children may also be admitted under the same visa category so long as these are also Canadian nationals. If the dependents are non-Canadians, they may be admitted as B-2 visitors.

A Canadian citizen in this classification may be readmitted to the United States for the remainder of the period authorized on the original form I-94 which he/she received at the border at the time of the initial entry, without presentation of the original letter or documentation. A Canadian admitted under this section may apply for an extension of stay on Form I-539, which form is standard for requests of extensions of stay. The application for extension shall be accompanied by a letter(s) from the United States employer(s) confirming the continued need for the Canadian citizen's services and stating the length of additional time needed.

A request to change U.S. employers is also made on the Form I-539, which must then be accompanied by a letter from the new employer describing the services to be performed, the time needed to render such services, and the terms of remuneration for services. Employment with a different or with an additional employer is not authorized prior to INS approval of the request for extension of stay.

In addition, the FTA provides for a procedure that allows for certain Canadian business persons to enter the United States temporarily. This would enable these persons to enter the United States for the purpose of extending performance of after sales, service and training to the life of a warranty or service agreement.

A Canadian is permitted to present an I-129 petition with supporting documentation, at a U.S. port of entry, rather than having the petition approved in advance at a local or regional Immigration & Naturalization office. Since these visa petitions generally require much documentation, it is recommended that an individual appear at the border at least three hours in advance of scheduled departure.

3.4 - THE L VISA. This visa, also known as the <u>Intra-company Transferee visa</u>, is one of the most flexible and sought-after temporary visas which provide for employment.

Section 101(a)(15)(L) of the Immigration and Nationality Act establishes the requirements for the L visa which is one of the most useful non-immigrant visas available to employees of foreign companies. The purpose of the L visa is to facilitate the transfer of key employees to the United States from companies that are affiliated or related to United States corporations. This visa is very useful because it is not limited to specific countries with which the United States may have entered a treaty. Nationals of all countries are eligible, provided the specific qualifications for the visa are satisfied.

DURATION OF STAY. The L-1 visa has a duration of seven years for "Managers" and "Executives" and five years for persons of "specialized knowledge". The duration of stay is issued for an initial period of three years and may be extended for additional periods of two years.

3.4.a. - REQUIREMENTS FOR OBTAINING THE L-1 VISA

DURATION OF EMPLOYMENT: The employee that is to be transferred must have been continuously employed by the overseas (extra-United States) company for a period of at least one year out of the last three years prior to his entry into the United States. Short business or pleasure trips to the United States during the one year period will not disqualify the employee from the visa. However, extended trips or visits to the United States may be considered by the INS as an interruption of the one (1) year foreign employment requirement.

INTRA-COMPANY RELATIONSHIP. The prior employer/foreign company must be related to the U.S. company, either as a subsidiary, affiliate, or as a division. This unity of identity is satisfied by any of the above legal relationships, and must, in most cases, be documented to the INS. The documentation of the U.S.-foreign corporation relationship may not need to be documented in the case of large, well-known multi-national corporation such as **Ford Motor Company, Monsanto, Dupont,** etc.

In order to establish that the foreign-domestic entities are one and the same for immigration purposes, it is necessary that the corporations be controlled by the same person(s) (affiliate) or that one corporation controls the other (subsidiary). In order to document the above, one must show that the U.S. corporation owns at least 51% of the shares of the foreign corporation, or vice-versa, or in the alternative that the same stockholders own 51% of each of the corporations. Another alternative is to show that the foreign corporation is a branch or division of the U.S. corporation or vice-versa. The requirement of common control can be satisfied in certain instances, even where the controlling entity does not own 51% of the stock. Thus, where a person owns less than 51% of the foreign corporation, he must show he has effective control of the corporation through legal documents, contracts, or some other documented arrangement.

The INS has taken the position that the degree and nature of ownership of the foreign and U.S. companies must be identical. That is, indirect ownership of either the foreign or domestic company by way of another company or business entity would, in the opinion of the INS disqualify either the U.S. or foreign company from filing a petition for an L-1 visa. This overly technical interpretation of the law has been rejected by at least one Federal court in the United States and it seems that the INS is backing away from this position. This is important, because for many foreign persons it is important that they not own real estate directly in their own name or perhaps even in a company once removed from ultimate beneficial ownership of the U.S. company. Nonetheless, where otherwise possible it would be beneficial to avoid tiers of ownership as between the U.S. affiliate and foreign parent that are different.

Let me give an example. A Taiwanese family owns 75% interest in a Taiwanese manufacturing concern. The same family acquires a U.S. company, but instead of owning it in the same fashion as they own the Taiwanese parent, the family forms two foreign holding corporations (organized in the country of Barbados) which in turn own all the stock in the U.S. affiliate company. Even though the family indirectly own the U.S. affiliate company in the same proportion as they own the Taiwanese company, the INS may make a technical objection on the basis that the forms of ownership of the companies differ. This pedantic attitude on the part of the INS may change on this subject matter, but as of the writing of this book, it represents the current posture of the INS. The reason why a foreign person may decide to hold U.S. business and real property interests using a multi-tiered corporate structure may be due to sound tax and other reporting requirement concerns, but there is no automatic understanding or acceptance by the INS of these other very valid motivations.

In addition, the petitioning company must continue to be a "qualifying organization". Thus, the foreign company must continue to function as a viable business entity throughout the employment period of the L-1 visa holder. If the foreign entity ceases to exist or to function as a viable business entity, then the L-visa status of the employee is jeopardized. This is an extremely important point for a small company to bear in mind.

EMPLOYEE'S QUALIFICATIONS. The law defines "manager," "executive" and "person of specialized knowledge" as follows:

Manager: (a) Primarily manages the organization, or a department, subdivision, function, or component of the organization. The addition of the concept "function" gives the definition more usefulness for smaller companies or companies in which a key function is primarily managed and run by the same person.

(b) Primarily supervises and controls the work of other supervisory, professional or managerial employees, or manages an essential function within the organization, or a department or subdivision of the organization. In order to qualify as a "manager" under these regulations, a first line supervisor must supervise professional persons. Thus, a manager would not qualify as such if he is the first line supervisor of actual production personnel.

(c) Has the authority to hire and fire or recommend those as well as other personnel actions if another employee or other employees are supervised; if no other employees are supervised, functions at a senior level within the organizational hierarchy or with respect to the function managed; and

(d) Exercises discretion over the day-to-day operations of the activity or function for which the employee has authority.

Executive: (a) Directs the management of the organization or a major component or function. Note that this is similar to subsection (c) under "Manager" as defined above,

(b) Establishes the goals and policies of the organization, component, or function;

(c) Exercises wide latitude in discretionary decision-making; and

(d) Receives only general supervision or direction from higher level executives, the board of directors or stockholders of the organization.

Person of Specialized Knowledge: (a) Must have special or unique knowledge of the petitioning organization's product, service, research, equipment, techniques, management or other interests and its application in international markets, or an advanced level of knowledge or expertise in the organization's processes and procedures.

(b) "Special Knowledge" is knowledge which is different from or exceeds the ordinary or usual knowledge of an employee in a particular field.

(c) a specialized knowledge professional is a person who has specialized knowledge and is a member of the professions.

There is no requirement that the position to be filled by the employee be identical to that abroad, or that it have all of the same responsibilities, but the position in the United States must be at least of the equivalent classification as the position of the employee abroad.

3.4.b. - NEWLY FORMED COMPANIES.

The purpose of the law, originally, was to provide for the transfer to the United States of managers and key persons from and by multinational corporations. However, the letter of the law as written also permits small companies to benefit from the L visa, even companies that are composed of no more than two or three individuals.

The INS regulations have the following additional requirements for newly formed companies. A "newly formed company" is one which has been in business for less than one year. A newly formed U.S. company which is a subsidiary or affiliate of a foreign company must establish that it has obtained a place for conducting business and, that the beneficiary had been employed abroad as a manager or executive and will continue in that capacity in the U.S. If the beneficiary is a major stockholder of the company proof must be submitted that the employee will be transferred abroad at the completion of his temporary duties in the U.S.

All of the above points must be minutely documented to the INS. Indeed, one should provide, among other things, copies of the lease for the premises, copies of any business contracts, a cash projection for the business, copies of accounting and bank records to indicate that both the foreign company and the U.S. parent are viable entities. This usually takes the form of proof that the U.S. entity has the financial ability to cover the transferee's salary for at least the first year of operation. The petition, together with the supporting documentation, must then be filed with the appropriate district office of the INS for processing. I cannot overemphasize the importance of presenting a well organized and complete set of corroborating documents together with the Form I-129. I suggest that the reader review the instruction sheet for the Form I-129 which is attached as an Appendix to this book. The success or failure of the petition will be based for the most part on the strength of the documentary evidence submitted in support of the petition. After approval of the petition, the employee may bring the letter of approval to the nearest U.S. consular post for the issuance of the visa.

The purpose of this regulation is to prevent the sole owner (or his immediate relative) of a relatively small company from sponsoring a visa for him/herself where the real intention is to immigrate permanently to the United States. The regulation however, ignores economics and business realities and again requires a mechanistic view of a business organization.

The regulations further state that in defining "executive or managerial" for L visa purposes the INS will review the size of the company and the total number of employees employed by the company. The regulations seem to be creating an additional requirement of size and or structure that is not contained in the original law and is subject to attack in the court systems. This new development requires close study and analysis by any foreign company seeking to expand operation into the United States.

COMPANY MUST BE "DOING BUSINESS": IMMACT90 also requires that the petitioning company be in the business of providing regular, systematic and continuous goods and/or services and specifically does not include the mere presence of an agent or office of the qualifying organization in the U.S. and abroad. The law clearly favors entrepreneurial activities rather than passive investments. Indeed, if the person is not needed to actively manage or supervise a key function of the organization, he probably does not need to be physically present in the United States -- or at least that is the attitude of the government on this issue.

ALIEN'S INTENT. An important consideration for this visa (as is the case with all of the others discussed in this book) is the question of intent. This applies to the employer and the employee. In both cases, it is required that the intention be one of a temporary nature. The INS regulations interpreting the L-1 (and H-1B visa) visa requirements now clearly state that the filing of a permanent visa petition by the alien does not negate the temporary intention required for the issuance of the L-1 visa. Thus, it seems that at least as concerns the L-1 and H-1B visas the perennial problem of temporary intent vs. permanent intent has been eliminated. The mere statement of intention by the employee or alien that the alien intends to depart the United States at the conclusion of the L-1 visa stay should be sufficient to satisfy the intention requirement.

However, the focus of attention will now be on the qualifications of the alien. While this may seem to be a vast improvement in the processing of these visas experience indicates that it may not get any easier to obtain the visa just because the intent question has been resolved. I fear that the INS as well as the STATE DEPARTMENT, acting through the U.S. consul abroad may increase their attention on the other eligibility requirements of the L-1 visa, so that the net result may be that it will be just as difficult to obtain this visa as before. It is my feeling that an alien applicant for the L-1 visa should preserve as many indicia of his intention to depart the United States upon the completion of the purpose of the entry to the United States under the L-1 visa.

Concerning the employee, the INS will look for indications of a true temporary intention. This visa does not require that the foreign employee maintain a home abroad, but if he does it is obviously helpful on the issue of temporariness.

The reason for this high degree of scrutiny by the INS concerning the L-1 visa is that, at least with respect to executives and managers, the issuance of the L-1 visa lends itself to a relatively easy conversion to a permanent visa. Normally, an alien must have received a job offer from a U.S. employer which has been certified by the Department of Labor as not displacing qualified local workers or negatively affecting the U.S. labor market. This process can take a long time. A manager or executive who holds an L-1 visa can probably qualify for a permanent visa as First Preference employment visa as a multinational manager or executive without the necessity of a labor certification. This is a highly coveted advantage.

It is accepted that an alien can have a "dual intent" with respect to his intention of the duration of stay. The employer and alien may have the intention of remaining in the United States on a temporary basis in compliance with the requirements of the L-1 visa while and still have an intention to file a petition for a permanent visa at some point in the future. Thus, putting the intention into words it can be thought of as saying the following: "It is my intention to remain in the United States on a temporary basis during the period of time that my L-1 visa is valid. I may decide to remain in the United States as a permanent resident by filing an application for a permanent visa, but I agree that I will depart the United States in the event that the L-1 visa expires before I obtain my permanent visa."

As a result of the long time delays in obtaining a permanent visa, an employee may need to extend his L visa before the permanent visa is approved. A new policy determination by the INS as of the writing of this book states that the filing of a request for labor certification or of a petition for a permanent visa will not "per se" disqualify a person from obtaining an extension to the L visa. In other words, the Immigration and Naturalization will look at other evidence to determine whether or not at the time a person applies for an extension of his L visa, he has a true intention to return to his home country in the event that the permanent visa is denied. To further complicate this quagmire of intention, it is still considered a fraud for a person to utilize the L visa for entry to the United States if his immediate and primary intention is to apply for a permanent visa in the future.

Even though at first glance the distinction between "dual intent" and a preconceived permanent intent may be somewhat, it must be thoroughly understood by the employee and the employer in order to avoid difficulties with the INS. This is especially the case where the person is the employee of a small business or a business in which he or she has a substantial interest.

3.4.c. - CHANGE OF STATUS FROM OTHER NON-IMMIGRANT CLASSIFICATION TO THE L-1 VISA.

If the alien is already in the United States and otherwise qualifies for the L-1 visa, he or she may elect to file for a Change of Status while he or she is in the United States so as to avoid the necessity of a trip abroad to a U.S. Consulate. Form I-506 is used to request this change of status. When a person holding a B-1 visa files for a Change of Status for purposes of establishing the office, and he has been in the United States for an extended period, there may be an interruption of the one-year foreign employment that is required.

As a result of the legal complexity concerning the requirements of the L visa, the employer and/or employee should seek the advice and counsel of a qualified immigration attorney before any definite steps are taken.

TEMPORARY WORKERS

3.5 - H-1A VISA (Professional Nurses). Most states in the United States are experiencing a shortage of qualified nurses. Consequently, the federal government has enacted a visa category specifically for registered nurses in order to help alleviate this problem. The H-1A non-immigrant visa is available to foreign nationals who (a) are otherwise qualified to practice as "registered nurses" in the state of destination in the United States or who (b) have passed the Commission on Graduates of Foreign Nursing Schools Examination (CGFNS).

In order to prove that the nurse is qualified to practice as a Registered Nurse, the person must establish that he/she has obtained a full and unrestricted license to practice nursing in the country where the person obtained his/her nursing education. In addition, the foreign person must establish that he/she has obtained a full and unrestricted license to practice as a Registered Nurse in the state of intended employment or has obtained a full and unrestricted license in <u>any</u> state or territory of the United States and has received temporary authorization to practice as a registered nurse in the state of intended employment. An additional requirement is that the nurse must be eligible to practice as a registered nurse in the state of intended employment immediately upon entry to the United States. The temporary license may be obtained immediately after the nurse enters the United States and registers to take the state examination for full licensure.

Nurses who enter the United States after passing the CGFNS must be eligible to receive temporary authorization to practice as a registered nurse in the state of intended employment after admission to the United States and then must take and pass the first available licensure examination in the state of intended employment.

DURATION OF STAY - The H-1A visa permits a total stay of five years with the possibility of an additional sixth year of stay in extraordinary circumstances. As of the date of publication of this book it was not clear as to whether the visa would be issued initially for the full term of five years or whether it would be granted in two or three year increments. In any event, this portion of the law will be subject to change based upon labor market conditions in the United States for registered nurses.

The Petitioning employer, in order to employ a foreign person as a registered nurse pursuant to the above law, must file a "Health Care Facility Attestation" with the United States Department of Labor at the applicable regional office in the state. Since this book is geared to the foreign person, the author has elected not to elaborate on the requirements imposed upon the Petitioning employer. For our purposes here, it is enough to say that the health care facility (which includes private households) must file an attestation with the Department of Labor which seeks to establish that the local labor market for nurses will not be adversely affected by the hiring of foreign nurses.

After the petitioning employer has filed its Health Care Facility Attestation and all the other requirements have been met, it may then file the visa petition itself on form I-129 with the regional service center of the Immigration and Naturalization Service. Upon approval, the INS issues a form I-171C which is then forwarded to the U.S. Consulate in the country of the alien nurses' nationality for visa issuance. If the nurse is already in the United States and is in status on her applicable visa, a CHANGE OF STATUS application may be filed which, if approved, will eliminate the necessity to travel to the U.S. consulate abroad and will authorize the foreign nurse to commence working in the United States.

For Canadian nurses, the application is somewhat simpler. The Canadian nurse must establish that he/she has a full and unrestricted State/Provincial license to practice as a professional or registered nurse as well as authorization to work in the state of intended employment in the United States. The Canadian nurse does not have to file the form I-129, but must document Canadian nationality and employment in the United States in the capacity as a registered nurse. Documentation should consist of diplomas, certificates and licenses which establish the nurse's credentials. The application itself may be made at the border point of entry, but it is recommended that some form of advance notification be made by the foreign nurse in order to avoid delays, especially at the airport.

In all cases, the accompanying spouse and minor children are also admitted together with the registered nurse but they are not eligible to work.

3.6 ALIENS OF EXTRAORDINARY ABILITY -

3.6.a O-1 Visas: This is a new visa category created by IMMACT90 for aliens of extraordinary ability in the sciences, arts, education, business or athletics. For persons other than in the motion picture and television industry, extraordinary ability is shown by "sustained national or international acclaim". It appears that at least with respect to business, sciences and education, the standard for eligibility could be quite high - perhaps the equivalent of a Noble Prize winner.

In the case of foreign persons who are engaged in the motion picture and television industry, extraordinary ability is shown through a "demonstrated record of extraordinary achievement". The documentation required will include letters and print media articles of acclaim, copies of awards as well as portfolios indicating the nature and extent of the performer's activities.

Consultation with local industry groups - The law also requires that the INS consult with union and management groups in the motion picture and television industry on an advisory basis, prior to issuance or denial of the visa. The recently promulgated rule of the INS provides that petitioners for both O and P aliens must obtain an advisory opinion before submitting the petition. If the petition lacks the advisory opinion then, the INS will ask a peer group or labor union for an advisory opinion only if the INS agrees that the petition merits expeditious handling. If the INS does not feel that the case merits expeditious handling then it will deny the petition. Needless to say, the INS is generally not sympathetic to the custom and usage in the entertainment industry pertaining to last minute scheduling and promotion and a petition should also provide proof as to the expeditious nature of the contracting arrangement. The attitude of many of the INS personnel is that the failure of the petitioner to plan properly does not mandate that the INS adopt a "crisis" approach to the adjudication of the petition. There is some logic to this position.

The INS rules provide that a labor union or peer group must act on an INS request for an advisory opinion within fifteen (15) days after receiving a copy of the petition.

In the event there is no union or other "peer" group with which to consult, the INS may issue the visa without such consultation. The law is an improvement over the prior practice under the old H-1 regulations which did not provide for consultation with management groups. The advisory opinions by unions or management groups which recommend denial must be in writing and the INS must attach those to its final decision.

Duration - There is a three (3) year limitation on the initial duration of this visa. The duration of the visa shall be sufficient for the completion of the event(s) or activity. Extensions of stay are granted only in order to complete the event(s) or activity but in no event for longer than three years.

Standards for "Extraordinary Ability" - The administrative Code of Federal Regulations establishes the standards for determining extraordinary ability as follows:

"1) Receipt of a major internationally recognized award such as the Nobel Prize, or

2) At least three of the following forms of documentation:

a) Documentation of the alien's receipt of nationally or internationally recognized prizes or awards for excellence in their field of endeavor.

b) Documentation of the alien's membership and association in the field for which classification is sought which require outstanding achievement of their members as judged by recognized national or international experts in their disciplines or fields.

c) Published material in professional or major trade publications or major media about the alien relating to the alien's work in the field for which classification is sought which shall include the title, date and author of such published material and any necessary translation.

d) Evidence of the alien's participation on a panel or individually as a judge of the work of others in the same or in an allied field of specialization to that for which classification is sought.

e) Evidence of the alien's original scientific scholarly or business related contributions of major significance in the field.

f) Evidence of the alien's authorship of scholarly articles in the field in professional journals or other major media.

g) Evidence that the alien has been employed in a critical or essential capacity for organizations and establishments that have a distinctive reputation.

h) Evidence that the alien has commanded and/or commands a high salary or other remuneration for services evidenced by contracts or other reliable evidence."

The INS has promulgated the final rules establishing the standards for determining extraordinary achievement or extraordinary ability in the arts. They are reproduced from the Federal Register (Vol. 57, No. 69, April 9, 1992) as follows:

"(A) Evidence that the alien has been nominated for or has been the recipient of significant national or international awards or prizes in the particular field such as Academy Award, an Emmy, a Grammy, or a Directors Guild Award: or (B) At least three of the following forms of documentation:

(1) Evidence that the alien has performed and will perform services as a lead or starring participant in productions or events which have a distinguished reputation as evidenced by critical reviews, advertisements, publicity releases, publications, contracts, or endorsements;

(2) Evidence that the alien has achieved national or international recognition for achievements evidenced by critical reviews or other published materials by or about the individual in major newspapers, trade journals, magazines, or other publications;

(3) Evidence that the alien has performed in a lead, starring, or critical role for organizations and establishments that have a distinguished reputation evidenced by articles in newspapers, trade journals.

(4) Evidence that the alien has a record of major commercial or critically acclaimed successes as evidenced by such indicators as title, rating, standing in the field, box office receipts, credit for original research or

product development, motion picture or television ratings, and other occupational achievements reported in trade journals, major newspapers, or other publications;

(5) Evidence that the alien has received significant recognition for achievements from organizations, critics, government agencies, or other recognized experts in the field in which the alien is engaged. Such testimonials must be in a form which clearly indicates the author's authority, expertise, and knowledge of the alien's achievements; or

(6) Evidence that the alien has commanded or now commands a high salary or other substantial remuneration for services in relation to others in the field, as evidenced by contracts or other reliable evidence; or

————

(C) If the above standards do not readily apply to the beneficiary's [alien] occupation, the petitioner may submit comparable evidence in order to establish the beneficiary's eligibility."

A recent opinion letter from the Acting INS Assistant Commissioner for Adjudications has opined that O-1 aliens can petition for themselves and, thus, do not need to be hired by a U.S. employer.

O-2 Visa - This visa is used for those foreign persons who accompany and/or assist the O-1 alien in the athletic or artistic performance. The person must be an integral part of the performance of the O-1 visa person and must have critical skills and experience with the O-1 alien that are not of a general nature and cannot be readily replicated by other individuals.

O-2 visa applicants who assist persons in the movie and television industry must have a pre-existing and long standing working relationship with the O-1 alien and, in the event of filming, must be needed for purposes of maintaining continuity of filming both inside and outside of the U.S.

Unlike the O-1 alien, the O-2 visa applicant must show that he/she has a foreign residence which he/she has no intention of abandoning and consultation is also required for this group, but only from labor organizations experienced in the skill involved. Depending on how the regulations are drafted, this requirement of consultation could result in delays and conflict, since the opinion of a labor organization and the principal O-1 alien could differ on the question of O-2 alien's importance to the O-1 visa holder.

Dependent family members of O-1 and 2 aliens are issued O-3 visas.

The P Visa - This visa is for two types of internationally recognized individuals:

a) Athletes who compete individually or as part of a team at an "internationally recognized level of performance"; and

b) Entertainers who perform as part of a group that has received international recognition as "outstanding" for a "sustained and substantial period of time". The INS has recently promulgated rules and regulations establishing the standards for these terms. They are reproduced as follows from the FEDERAL REGISTER (Vol. 57, No. 69, April 9, 1992):

"...A P-1 athlete must have an internationally recognized reputation as an international athlete or he or she must be a member of a foreign team that is internationally recognized. The athlete or team must be coming to the United States to participate in an athletic competition which has a distinguished reputation and which requires participation of an athlete or athletic team that has an international reputation.

(B) *Standards for an internationally recognized athlete or athletic team.* A petition for an athletic team must be accompanied by evidence that the team as a unit has achieved international recognition in the sport. Each member of the team is accorded P-1 classification based on the international reputation of the team. A petition for an athlete who will compete individually or as a member of a United States team must be accompanied by evidence that the athlete has achieved international recognition in the sport based on his or her reputation. A petition for a P-1 athlete or athletic team shall include:

(1) a tendered contract with a major United States sports league or team, or a tendered contract in an individual sport commensurate with international recognition in that sport, and

(2) Documentation of at least two of the following:

(i) Evidence of having participated to a significant extent in a prior season with a major United States sports league;

(ii) Evidence of having participated in international competition with a national team;

(iii) Evidence of having participated to a significant extent in a prior season for a United States college or university in intercollegiate competition;

(iv) A written statement from an official of a major United States sports league or an official of the governing body of the sport which details how the alien or team is internationally recognized;

(v) A written statement from a member of the sports media or a recognized expert in the sport which details how the alien or team is internationally recognized;

(vi) Evidence that the individual or team is ranked if the sport has international rankings; or

(vii) Evidence that the alien or team has received a significant honor or award in the sport.

(iii) *Criteria and documentary requirements for members of an international recognized entertainment group--(A) General.* A P-1 classification shall be accorded to an international group to perform as a unit based on the international reputation of the group. Individual entertainers shall not be accorded P-1 classification to perform separate and apart from a group. Except as provided in paragraph (p)(4)(iii)(C)(2) of this section, it must be established that the group has been internationally recognized as outstanding in the discipline for a sustained and substantial period of time.

-67-

Seventy-five percent [75%] of the members of the group must have had a sustained and substantial relationship with the group for at least one year and must provide functions integral to the group's performance.

(B) *Standards for members of internationally recognized entertainment groups.* A petition for P-1 classification for the members of an entertainment group shall be accompanied by:

(1) Evidence that the group, under the name shown on the petition, has been established and performing regularly for a period of at least one year;

(2) A statement from the petitioner listing each member of the group and the exact dates for which each member has been employed on a regular basis by the group; and

(3) Evidence that the group has been internationally recognized in the discipline. This may be demonstrated by the submission of evidence of he group's nomination or receipt of significant international awards or prizes for outstanding achievement in its field or by three of the following different types of documentation:

(i) Evidence that the group has performed and will perform as a starring or leading entertainment group in productions or events which have a distinguished reputation as evidenced by critical reviews, advertisements, publicity releases, publications, contracts, or endorsement.

(ii) Evidence that the group has achieved international recognition and acclaim for outstanding achievement in its field as evidenced by reviews in major newspapers, trade journals, magazines, or other published materials;

(iii) Evidence that the group has performed and will perform services as a leading or starring group for organizations and establishments that have a distinguished reputation evidenced by articles in newspapers, trade journals, publications, or testimonials;

(iv) Evidence that the group has a record of major commercial or critically acclaimed successes, as evidenced by such indicators as ratings, standing in the field, box office receipts, record, cassette, or video sales, and other achievements in the field as reported in trade journals, major newspapers, or other publications;

(v) Evidence that the group has achieved significant recognition for achievements from organizations, critics, government agencies, or other recognized experts in the field. Such testimonials must be in a form that clearly indicates the author's authority, expertise, and knowledge of the alien's achievements; or

(vi) Evidence that the group has commanded or now commands a high salary or other substantial remuneration for services comparable to others similarly situated in the field as evidenced by contracts or other reliable evidence.

(C) *Special provisions for certain entertainment groups.--(1) Alien circus personnel.* The one-year group membership requirement is not applicable to alien circus personnel who perform as part of a circus or circus group, or who constitute an integral and essential part of the performance of such circus or circus group, provided that the alien or aliens are coming to join a circus that has been recognized nationally as outstanding for a sustained and substantial period of time as part of such a circus.

---

(2) *Certain nationally known entertainment groups.* The director may waive the international recognition requirement in the case of an entertainment group which has been recognized nationally as being outstanding in its discipline for a sustained and substantial period of time in consideration of special circumstances. An example of a special circumstances would be when an entertainment group may find it difficult to demonstrate recognition in more than one country due to such factors as limited access to news media or consequences of geography."

The one year membership requirement may be waived if the new member is replacing another member because of illness or other exigent circumstances or in the event the new member augments the group by performing a critical role.

Note that entertainers who perform individually cannot be issued this visa.

In addition to the above, at least 25% of the P-1 entertainers must have had a "sustained and substantial" relationship with the group for a period of at least one year and all must provide integral functions to the group's performance.

The Attorney General of the United States acting through the District Director of the applicable Immigration and Naturalization District office may waive the "international" requirement or consider other types of evidence to sustain the substantial recognition factor for the entertainment group. This provision should benefit entertainment groups which may be quite talented and recognized in their country or region, but who do not yet have an international acclaim or recognition.

The P-2 Visa - This visa is issued to artists and entertainers who participate in an exchange program between a foreign based organization and a U.S. based organization which are engaged in the temporary exchange of artists and entertainers. This visa applies to both individuals and groups. Future administrative regulation will define the details for the eligibility and documentary requirements for these visas.

The P-3 Visa - This visa is applicable to artists and entertainers who perform "under a program that is culturally unique".

Duration of stay for the P Visa - The duration of stay under both P-2 and P-3 visas is the amount of time needed for the specific performance or event. P-1 athletes, however, may be allowed a duration of stay of up to ten years. This is a very sound provision since many professional athletes are required or encouraged to sign multi-year contracts with the team organizations for which they are playing.

Other requirements: P visa applicants must have a residence in a foreign country which they have no intention of abandoning. This requirement does not apply to O visa applicants and the foreign person must be entering to work in his/her respective field of endeavor.

3.6.f. H-1B Visa - This is one of the most important non-immigrant visas available to qualified foreign persons desiring to come to the United States in order to work. The administrative regulations defining this visa are as follows:

The "...H-1B classification applies to an alien who has come temporarily to the United States to perform services in a specialty occupation and for whom the Secretary of Labor has determined and certified to the Attorney General that the prospective employer has an approved labor condition application or to perform services of an exceptional nature requiring exceptional merit and ability relating to a cooperative research and development project of a co-production project provided for under a government to government agreement administered by the Secretary of Defense or to perform services of an exceptional nature requiring distinguished merit and ability as artists, entertainers, athletes, or fashion models; or to accompany and assist in the artistic or athletic performance by an alien who is admitted pursuant to H-1B status". (8 C.F.R. 214.29(h)(1)(ii)(B)(1-4).)

This visa is highly sought after because, unlike many other types of visas, the position being filled by the alien can be permanent. It is only the need for the alien that must be temporary. Furthermore, the foreign national is not required to have any prior employment experience with the same employer, nor does the employer have to be international in character.

Specialty Occupation - "This is an occupation which requires theoretical and practical application of a body of highly specialized knowledge to fully perform the occupation in such fields of human endeavor including, but not limited to, architecture, engineering, mathematics, physical sciences, medicine and health, education, business specialties, accounting, law, theology, and the arts, and which requires the attainment of a bachelor's degree or higher in a specific specialty, or its equivalent, as a minimum for entry into the occupation in the United States". This definition actually describes a classic profession which requires the application of a theoretical body of knowledge to particular circumstances.

Prominence is defined as a high level of achievement in the fields of arts, entertainment, athletics, or fashion modeling evidenced by a degree of skill and recognition substantially above that which is ordinarily encountered. A person described as prominent must be renowned, leading, or well known in the field of endeavor.

Employer's requirements - Before filing an H-1B petition, the prospective employer (petitioner) must file and have accepted a labor condition application with the Department of Labor. The labor condition application is essentially a representation that the petitioner has agreed to pay the H-1B beneficiary the prevailing wage for the job.

Employee's (Beneficiary) requirements for a Specialty Occupation - In order to qualify as a specialty occupation the beneficiary-employee must meet one of the following criteria:

a) Hold a United States Baccalaureate or higher degree required by the specialty occupation from an accredited college or university;

b) Hold a foreign degree determined to be equivalent to a United States Baccalaureate or higher degree required by the specialty occupation from an accredited college or university;

c) Hold an unrestricted state license, registration or certification which authorizes him or her to fully practice the specialty occupation and be immediately engaged in that specialty in the state of intended employment; or

1) If a temporary license is available and the foreign person is allowed to perform the duties of the occupation without a permanent license, and an analysis of the facts demonstrate that the alien under supervision is authorized to fully perform the duties of the occupation, H classification may be granted. This might be the case for certain health related occupations such as physical therapists, for which occupations a state might provide a temporary license pending completion of all requirements for permanent licensure.

2) In certain occupations which generally require licensure, a state may allow an individual to fully practice the occupation under the supervision of licensed supervisory personnel in that occupation. In such cases, if the facts demonstrate that the alien under supervision can fully perform the duties of the occupation, H classification will be granted. This might be the case, for example, with architects who are able to fully perform their functions as long as they work under the authorization of an employer architect's state license.

d) Have education, specialized training, and/or progressively responsible experience that is equivalent to completion of a United States Baccalaureate or higher degree in the specialty occupation, and have recognition of expertise in the specialty through progressively responsible positions directly related to the specialty.

Requirements for Aliens Claiming Distinguished Merit and Ability -

a) An alien of distinguished merit and ability must be one who is prominent in the field of art, entertainment, athletics, or fashion modeling and the alien must be coming to the United States to perform services which require a person of prominence. It is important to note that in addition to proving that the foreign person is indeed prominent, the law and the regulations require that the foreign person and the petitioner, ie., the employer, prove that the job requires a person with the high level of skill which the term "prominence" entails. In other words, the employer must establish some form of business necessity for requiring a person of prominence rather than just a desire to upgrade the job or to otherwise serve the convenience of the employer.

b) An approved labor condition application must accompany a petition for fashion modeling for H-1B classification.

A constant problem for persons applying for the H-1B visa claiming distinguished merit and ability is obtaining an opinion of equivalency for the foreign person's education and training abroad. The law now provides by administrative regulation several methods of obtaining equivalencies.

1) An evaluation from an official who has authority to grant college-level credit for training and/or experience in the specialty at an accredited college or university which has a program for granting such credit based on an individual's training and/or work experience;

2) The results of recognized college-level equivalency examinations or special credit programs, such as the College Level Examination Program (CLEP), or Program on Non-Collegiate Sponsored Instruction (PONSI);

3) An evaluation of education by a reliable credentials evaluation service which specializes in evaluating foreign educational credentials;

4) Evidence of certification or registration from a nationally recognized professional association in the specialty that is knows to grant certification or registration to persons who have achieved a certain level of competence;

5) A determination by INS that the equivalent of the degree required by the specialty occupation has been acquired through a combination of education, specialized training, and/or work experience in areas related to the specialty and that the alien has achieved recognition of expertise in the specialty occupation as a result of such training and experience. For purposes of determining equivalency to a baccalaureate degree in the specialty, three years of specialized training and/or work experience are required by the INS for each year of college level training the alien lacks. In addition, the INS requires that the alien produce at least one type of documentation such as recognition of expertise in the specialty occupation by at least two recognized authorities in the same specialty occupation; membership in a recognized foreign or United States association or society in the specialty occupation; published material by or about the alien in professional publications, trade journals, books, or major newspapers; licensure or registration to practice a specialty occupation in a foreign country; or achievements which a recognized authority has determined to be significant contributions to the field of the specialty occupation.

The INS has issued a new I-129 Petition which is used for all of the above visas, including the E-1/2 visas when a change of status is requested. The new form has attached a relatively clear and useful set of instructions. The instruction sheet is included in this book as Appendix A. Understand, however, that the form requires complete and accurate documentation in order to comprise a completed petition.

Duration of Stay - The H-1B visa is issued for three years and may be extended once. Foreign persons who are issued an H-1B visa in order to work on a Department of Defense project are issued a visa valid for five years.

Annual Quota - There is a maximum of 65,000 visas to be issued annually for this visa. This is the first time that a quota has been established for a non-immigrant visa.

Of course, the employer must always establish that it has the financial resources to pay the alien's salary and is otherwise a viable economic entity. If the alien is an owner or part owner of the business, he must convince the Immigration and Naturalization Service that his intention to remain in the United States is only temporary, regardless of his ownership interest in the company. If the company does not have other employees or is not otherwise a going enterprise then the H visa petition may be denied. Even though the Form I-129 is deceptively simple, the employer and employee must accompany the petition with substantial documentation to establish their intent, qualifications, and financial ability. The instruction sheet to form I-129 has been included in this book as an appendix and it is instructive to review it along with the material presented in this section.

Once the visa is obtained, it may be extended for an additional two-year period, which would provide for a maximum duration of stay of five years. In filing a request for the extension, the employer will have to justify why it needs to maintain the employee on a temporary basis for an additional two years, and the employee will have to prove that he still harbors a temporary intent and will, in fact, leave the United States as soon as the duration of stay of the visa expires. The filing of a labor certification by the H-1B foreign national, as the first step in a petition for a permanent visa, will not in and of itself disqualify the alien from obtaining the H-1B extension, but it will certainly cause the

Immigration and Naturalization Service to scrutinize his intention very carefully. The Immigration and Naturalization Service is very concerned that persons may utilize the H-1B visa as a stepping stone for a permanent visa and thus may not have a bona fide temporary intent. The employee must justify and explain to the INS that he or she truly intends to leave the United States at the termination of the duration of stay of the H-1B visa in the event he or she has not obtained his permanent visa status prior to that time the H-1 will expire. It must be borne in mind, however, that each case will be handled on an individual basis, and the INS will now be looking at factual and circumstantial evidence to determine what is the true intention of the employee and employer.

Physicians - The H-1B regulations now permit foreign physicians to enter the United States to practice medicine (direct patient care) under certain specified conditions. A foreign physician may perform direct patient care if he/she (1) has a license or other interim authorization otherwise required by the state of intended employment to practice medicine; and (2) has a full and unrestricted license to practice medicine in a foreign country or has graduated from a medical school in the United States or a foreign country.

If the physician is being admitted primarily to teach or conduct research for a public or nonprofit private educational or research institution, only condition (2) above mentioned needs to be complied with. As far as the petitioning employer is concerned, it must establish that the alien is coming to the United States primarily to teach or conduct research as described above or, if coming to provide patient care, has passed the **Federation Licensing Examination** (FLEX) examination and is competent in English or is a graduate of an accredited medical school. In order to demonstrate competency in English the alien must pass the English proficiency test given by the **Educational Commission for Foreign Medical Graduates** (ECGMG). This rule of the IMMIGRATION & NATURALIZATION SERVICE went into effect shortly before the date of publication of this book. Further details and experience in the implementation of these new rules will determine the feasibility of utilizing this visa category for aliens who intend to practice medicine in the United States, albeit on a temporary basis. It is possible to enter the United States with this visa and then adjust status to that of permanent residency if conditions and circumstances warrant.

EDUCATIONAL/TRAINING VISAS: This section will discuss one of three types of educational-training visas, which are available to qualified foreign persons. They all share the common purpose of serving to upgrade the education and/or vocation skills of foreign persons, but differ markedly in the approaches that are taken to fulfill these goals. Please read the following two chapters as a single unit with a comparative view.

3.7 - H-2 VISA(S). IMMACT90 subdivided the former H-2 Visa category into H-2A and H-2B. The H-2A visa applies to persons coming to the United States to perform agricultural work of temporary or seasonal nature. This is a specialized visa process and the INS has published a handbook which provides details to prospective farm employers on the requirements of this visa.

The H-2B visa applies to persons whose job skills or occupation do not rise to the level of an H-1B and who are coming to the United States to perform temporary work for a United States employer. The need for the employee must be temporary even though the job itself may not be of a temporary nature. Thus, if the employer needs a worker for a one time occurrence or to meet seasonal or intermittent needs, then the employer may hire the foreign person if he first obtains a labor certification from the Department of Labor to the effect that there are no U.S. persons available to perform the job requested and the employment of the alien will not adversely affect wages and working conditions of workers in the U.S. In fact, because of the expense and inconvenience involved in obtaining the labor certification, I personally do not feel that this visa category is very useful, at least in my experience. The visa is only issued for a one year period, so only a very unique position and circumstance would justify the expense and trouble involved in obtaining this visa.

This visa is used by U.S. companies to employ both skilled and unskilled aliens on a temporary basis. There are two parts of the "temporariness" concept which must be noted. First, the **position itself** that the alien is filling must be of a temporary nature, and secondly, the company's **need** for the designated position must also be temporary. This visa is issued for a duration of one year at a time and may be extended, with some difficulty, up to a maximum period of three years. Another feature of the H-2 visa which differentiates it from the H-1B visa is that a Department of Labor "certification" must usually be issued as a precondition to the issuance of the visa. This is a marked difference from the H-1 visa which does not require a Department of Labor certification.

ELIGIBILITY REQUIREMENTS. Most of the eligibility requirements for this visa pertain to the employer, rather than the employee, even though the alien employee must be qualified for the position for which he is being hired. As previously stated, a United States employer is required to file a request for a labor certification from the Department of Labor as a prerequisite to the filing of an H-2B petition. It is incumbent upon the employer to prove to the Department of Labor that there are no U.S. workers available in the location of the job offering who are willing and able to perform the required work at current and prevailing wage rates. In addition, the employer will need to prove that the employment of the alien workers will not adversely affect the U.S. labor market.

The procedure outlined above is identical to the procedure required for a Department of Labor certification for an immigrant visa except that the Department of Labor is only interested in Part A of the Labor Certification request, which deals with the employer's needs and job offering. Part B of the ETA-750 which lists the alien's qualifications, does not have to be completed. If the Department of Labor denies the certification it is still possible to obtain the H-1B visa if the employer can convince the INS as to the unavailability of local labor to perform the job. This is not an easy task and, frankly, is probably not worth the effort.

TEMPORARINESS. Assuming that the Department of Labor issues a labor certification, the employer must still prove to the satisfaction of the Immigration and Naturalization Service that the need for the position is temporary and that the position itself is temporary. An example of these conditions is where the United States employer commences a new manufacturing operation and requires the assistance of a foreign expert who can train the employer's existing U.S. workers and give consulting advice to the management on the organization and administration of the new operation. In this example, the position is temporary in that it has a defined ending and a defined beginning and the need is temporary since the employer's need will terminate with the completion of the job.

It is important to note that the mere designation of a termination date is insufficient proof of "temporariness" to the Immigration and Naturalization Service. Rather, it is required that the employer give operational evidence as to the projected termination of the position as well as the employer's need for that position in order to support the visa.

ALIEN'S QUALIFICATIONS. In order for the alien to be the beneficiary of the H-2 petition, he must establish his qualifications to perform the job requested. The job may be skilled or unskilled and can range from a high degree of technological expertise to that of a seasonal unskilled laborer. In any event, the alien must prove that he is qualified by work experience or training or both to perform the job.

In addition, the alien must prove that his intention in entering the United States is temporary, and that he maintains a home in a foreign country to which he intends to return as soon as his job tour is over.

SPECIAL PROBLEMS. It is nearly impossible to adjust the H-2 Visa to that of a permanent resident alien. The Immigration and Naturalization Service has consistently maintained in a series of judicial and administrative rulings that the initial certification by an employer that the position as well as the employer's need were temporary, preclude a later contention that the same position and need has now changed to that of permanent nature. In essence, the Immigration and Naturalization Service treats the initial petition as a warranty by the employer that the temporary character of the position will not change in the future to that of a permanent position to justify the employment of the alien. It is possible for an employer to file a permanent visa petition or a petition to change the status on behalf of an employee's temporary visa so long as it is for a different employment position with different responsibilities than those which formed the basis for the issuance of the original H-2 visa.

APPLICATION REQUIREMENTS. The application for an H-2 visa, as indicated above, consists of essentially two steps. The first is the completion of the Department of Labor certification by the employer, and the second is the processing of the actual petition via Form I-129 by the employer with the Immigration and Naturalization Service. It is not necessary that the employer actually obtain the Department of Labor certification as a prerequisite to the issuance of the H-2 visa. That is, if the labor certification request is denied, the employee may offer rebuttal evidence to the Immigration and Naturalization Service, together with the letter of denial by the Department of Labor and attempt to persuade the Immigration and Naturalization Service to issue the visa, notwithstanding the Department of Labor denial. The Immigration and Naturalization Service, however, normally gives much weight and credence to the finding of the Department of Labor in these matters.

ISSUANCE OF THE H-2 VISA. In the event the visa is granted, then the Immigration and Naturalization Service will issue its approval notice on Form I-171C, which is sent to the employer. The employer will then forward this original form, together with its petition to the appropriate U.S. Consulate abroad. The U.S. Consulate will then make a file for the beneficiary (or beneficiaries) and issue the individual visas. The petition filed by the employer can be for multiple workers for the same position.

DURATION OF TIME AND EXTENSION PROCESS. The H-2 visa is granted for a one-year period and may be extended for additional periods of one year to a maximum of three years. The extension request is accomplished by filing an additional Form I-129, which is now used as an extension application, and an additional Department of Labor certification and additional filing fee.

Obviously, the necessity of having to go through a second Department of Labor certification militates against extending the H-2 Visas beyond the original one-year period. It is very difficult to file successfully a change of non-immigrant status from a different non-immigrant classification to H-2 classification. The likelihood that an alien who is in the United States in another nonimmigrant status would coincidentally discover a temporary job for which he is immediately qualified is rare. The reverse, however, is not as difficult, in that it may be possible to change an H-2 visa to that of a different non-immigrant classification as long as the beneficiary is eligible for that visa, and the visa is for a totally different position from that which supported the H-2 petition.

3.8 - H-3 VISA. This visa is offered to qualified foreign trainees who enter the United States with the purpose of participating in an established occupational training program. The visa anticipates that the alien will not be entering the United States for the purpose of engaging in productive employment, even though some degree of productive employment may be permissible so long as it is incidental to the trainee and is otherwise in consequential in nature.

ELIGIBILITY. Most of the eligibility requirements pertain to the U.S. company or entity under whose employment the alien will be entering the United States. In order to support an H-3 visa, the United States company must file a preliminary petition with the Immigration and Naturalization Service to participate in an established training and/or educational program. If the company does not have its own approved and fully structured in-house training program, then it will have to seek the assistance of one or more blanket agencies which have already been authorized by the United States Information Agency to sponsor the entry of qualified foreign persons as J-1 trainees. Training of the foreign persons cannot anticipate an eventual job offer by the U.S. employer. The law assumes that the H-3 visa holder will undergo training which will be useful in the alien's home country. The documentary proof must show that the employer is not seeking to train the foreign person for eventual U.S. employment, but rather for employment abroad.

In addition to the above, the U.S. employer must prove that the type of training which it offers the alien is unavailable in the alien's home country. This very often can be established by showing that the U.S. company's activities in the United States (or even on a worldwide basis) are unique.

The alien must prove that his intention is to enter the United States only for a temporary period of time and that he will return to a home or foreign domicile which he has no intention of abandoning.

Duration of the Visa. This H-3 visa is valid for the documented length of the approved training program which usually means an outside limit of two years. It is technically possible to extend the visa beyond a two-year period of time, but such a request will generally be met with skepticism by the Immigration and Naturalization Service. Where a number of foreign trainees will be undergoing the same training, it is possible to include all of them in a single petition filed by the U.S. company or training agency. The U.S. employer must establish that the majority of time spent by the alien in the United States will be a bona fide training-instructional program, as opposed to on-the-job productive employment. If, from a description of the position and its attentive duties, it seems as if the employer is gaining direct benefits from the foreign persons' activities in the United States, then the H Visa may be denied.

3.9 - THE F-1 VISA. This visa is available to persons who seek to enter the United States for the purpose of engaging in a full time academic program. The visa extends to persons enrolled at the elementary school level through the post-graduate and doctoral level of university education. In theory, the requirements for obtaining a visa are simple and straight forward. However, it is often difficult for persons from certain countries where there is high incidence of visa fraud to obtain this visa.

Duration of Stay. The F visa is granted for a period of stay known as "duration of status" ("DS"). That is, the visa is valid for the entire period of the proposed academic program. If an individual enrolls in a four-year college program leading to an engineering degree, the visa will be valid for the entire four-year university program, so long as he otherwise maintains his status and does not violate the terms of the visa. Upon the completion of the academic program, which serves as the basis for the visa, the foreign student must then apply for an extension of that visa if he decides to pursue an additional course of study. If a student changes institutions before the completion of the academic program, an extension application is not required even though the Immigration and Naturalization Service must be notified of the change.

Conditions of Eligibility. The foreign student must be coming to the United States to engage in a full time course of study, all of which is defined by regulations. In general, it requires a minimum of twelve semester or credit hours on the university level or equivalent assuming that the university considers this to be a full time course of study and charges a full time tuition therefor. For secondary or elementary grade school programs, the student must be enrolled in a course of study which the institution normally considers as a minimum in order to obtain the diploma. Enrollment in associate degree institutions is also acceptable to support an F visa so long as the student is involved in a full time course of study which usually requires a minimum of twelve hours.

Since the institution will be certifying on Form 1-20A that the student is in fact enrolled in a full time course of study, that certification is almost always accepted by the Department of State as proof that the full time course of study requirement will be met.

Visa Processing. In order to obtain the F visa, the student must apply for and receive admission to an approved educational institution in the United States. In addition to any other matriculation documentation, the student will also receive a completed Form I-20A-B which will be filled out by the school and will require very little information from the student other than his signature in two places. Most information on Form I-20A-B has been provided by the student so the student should review it to make sure that it is accurate. The existing Form I-20A-B is an eight-page document which is submitted to the Visa Office at the time the student applies for his visa. In addition, the student will prepare and execute Form OF-156, which is a general non-immigrant visa application form. It is important that all questions are properly answered and particularly those questions from pages 19 through 30 properly reflect the student's temporary intention.

Exception to the Above Procedure. Occasionally a prospective student will not have yet chosen a particular institution at which he will study and may enter the United States on a B-2 visa, and then make a change of non-immigrant visa after he has made his selection. In this case, the student will appear before the visa officer and prove his student intention and financial ability and may then receive a B-2 visa which will be stamped "prospective student/school not chosen". This will be very helpful when the student later files an application to change his status after he has chosen his school. This notation is very important because without it, the student may find it very difficult to change his status to that of an F visa from a tourist visa. That is because the Immigration and Naturalization Service very often considers these change requests as evidence that the prospective student entered the United States on a fraudulent basis (preconceived intent), bypassing the normal F visa application process. A notation will thus avoid that problem since it will establish that there has been no fraud on the visa officer.

Persons seeking to enter the United States under F visa status must present a valid passport with the F visa stamped therein, together with Form I-20A-B. The student will then be examined at the border with respect to the school that he will be attending and the duration of the program. If the immigration officer is satisfied that the person is entitled to the F visa, then he will give the student the I-94 arrival/departure record with the notation "DS" stamped therein, which means Duration of Status, and will also return a portion of the I-20 form (i.d. copy), both of which documents the alien must keep. Certain types of on-campus employment are permissible if it is the type of employment that is normally done by students and does not displace U.S. labor. Thus, the position of library or laboratory assistant employment is permissible. We have included in the Appendix sample of Forms I-20A-B and Form OF-156.

Eligible Institutions. In order to qualify for the F visa, the student must be enrolled in an institution which has been approved for that purpose by the Attorney General. All public elementary, secondary, and post-secondary institutions are approved by the Attorney General, and most private institutions with established reputations and recognizable names are also approved. When applying for enrollment in an educational institution, unless it is public, the alien should inquire whether the private institution is in fact approved by the Attorney General. The student must be enrolled in an educational program that provides academic training as opposed to purely vocational-type training. A vocational or business school whose curriculum is basically non-academic would not support an F visa.

Financial Requirements. A prospective student must prove to the U.S. consul abroad that he or she has sufficient funds to pay for the educational training as well as to maintain himself during the duration of the program. This requirement very often causes great difficulty to applicants for this visa. The funds must be currently available, and not be based upon some speculative expectation of funding by the student. In this regard, the Department of State (the Visa Office) will want proof that the student, himself or through his family, has sufficient funds to pay the expenses. When a student has family or close friends who agree to provide room and board, an affidavit to this effect supported by proof of their financial stability would be very helpful. IMMACT90 provides for a pilot (temporary) program which permits the prospective student to engage in part time employment during his/her course of study in positions which do not displace U.S. labor. This is an exception to the general rule which prohibits F-2 students from gainful employment. In general, the foreign student cannot project anticipated earnings from part-time or full-time employment as a means of support during the educational program. If the prospective student is married, the spouse can accompany the F-1 visa holder but is not permitted to work. The only exception to this rule occurs if the financial circumstances that were reasonably relied upon by the alien change unexpectedly. In this case the student would have to make an application in the United States for permission to work.

English Language Proficiency. The student must be proficient in the English language or must be enrolled in a course of study that will enable proficiency in English. These matters are all covered in Form I-20A-B, which is filled out by the educational institution, which serves as a prerequisite for the issuance of the visa.

Temporary Intent-Proof. Perhaps the largest stumbling block for persons applying for the F visa is the requirement that the person have a purely temporary intent, and that he/she have a domicile to which he shall return at the completion of the educational program. This requirement can cause great difficulty to persons who are of modest financial means, young, and are traveling to the United States alone, or at least without immediate family. Under these circumstances the Department of State is concerned that the individual may be entering the United States only for the purpose of employment and will disappear into the U.S. economy as soon as he/she leaves the airport. It is highly recommended that when a student is interviewed by the visa officer of the U.S. consulate, in addition to the required documents, such as Form I-20A-B and the other non-immigrant visa petition documents, that the student also bring with him documentary proof of his ties to his home country to substantiate his temporary intent. In this regard, family photographs and information as to membership in various civic and social organizations would be important. Perhaps proof that the student will be returning to a job at the completion of his studies, or any other evidence of ties to the home country would be very helpful.

Practical Training. A student may also apply for a period of practical training which cannot exceed the aggregate of twelve months, including time spent in practical training during the normal course of the student's academic training, such as summer vacations, mid-semester breaks, etc. The requirements essentially are that the practical training be related to the course of study of the alien's educational training in the United States, and that the student be unable to receive his practical training in his home country. In both instances, this is a matter of documentary proof and the Immigration and Naturalization Service will have to rule on the application. In general, the fact that a school official will certify by affidavit that the practical training sought by the student will be beneficial to his academic training is normally sufficient. In this regard, Form I-538 must be filled out, together with documentary information as to the unavailability of that type of training in the student's home country.

3.10 - THE J-1 VISA. An alien can enter the U.S. in J-1 status if (s)he has a residence abroad which he has not intention of abandoning and is a "bona fide student, scholar, trainee, teacher, professor, research assistant, specialist, or leader in a specialized knowledge or skill, or other person of similar description who is coming temporarily to the United States as a participant in a program designated by the Director of the United States Information Agency, for the purpose of teaching, instructing or lecturing, studying, observing, conducting research, consulting, demonstrating special skills, or receiving training and who, if he is coming to the United States to participate in a program under which he will receive graduate medical education or training, also meets the requirements of section 212 (j), and the alien spouse and minor children of such alien if accompanying him or following to join him."

This visa category permits a wide range of activities within the United States as long as the U.S. sponsor is part of an approved U.S.I.A. exchange program. Academic students are permitted to engage in a period of practical training for up to 18 months after the completion of the academic program. Trainees may obtain on-the-job training in a specialized filed of knowledge or skill for periods not to exceed 18 months. Employment is permitted in this visa category as long as the main focus of the employment activity is the development of skills by the foreign trainee. This visa category assumes that the foreign employee will be actively engaged in on-the-job training under employment circumstances equivalent to that of a U.S. employee in the same position. In other words, the U.S. employer may gain some productive benefits from the foreign employee's activities as long as the main purpose of the employee's presence in the United States is to gain on-the-job, practical training. This visa program is administered by the United States Information Agency.

Aliens may enter the United States to teach in specified schools offering the kind of specialized instruction within the alien's expertise. of the foreign individual

This visa is very often used for the purposes of bringing "au pairs" to the United States. This program envisions that the young foreign person will come to the United States to live and study in an approved family environment which will enhance the alien's knowledge and understanding of U.S. culture. Such a person typically lives with a U.S. family and provides certain minimum domestic duties in exchange for a modest stipend.

FOREIGN MEDICAL GRADUATES: This visa is also used for advanced courses of training such as medical school graduates. The alien medical graduate (physician) must have at least passed Parts I and II of the National Board of Medical Examiners Examination or the Foreign Medical Graduate Examination in Medical Sciences (FMGEMS).

The recently promulgated regulations implementing the new H-1B visa category provides a sound alternative to the J-1 visa for foreign medical graduates in that an alien may engage in full-time professional, clinical employment if: (1) (s)he has passed the FLEX or equivalent examination as may be established by the U.S. Department of Health and Human Services, (2) has obtained ECFMG English language certification and (3) is licensed by the state of intended employment. Such a medical graduate may also engage in graduate medical training and does not have to contend with the 2 year foreign residency requirement.

Duration of Stay. The duration of stay of the J-1 visa is limited to the time required to complete the program for which (s)he was admitted. Students and medical technologists may remain for the duration of their program plus eighteen months of practical training. Graduate medical students may remain for up to seven years. Business and industrial trainees may remain for a maximum of eighteen months.

Eligibility. Again, most of the eligibility requirements focus on the U.S. employer to determine whether or not the sponsor has been designated by the United States Information Agency as an exchange-visitor program sponsor. Thus, a company, if it is has its own established program, may seek to bring foreign employees to the United States in accordance with its already-approved program. In the event it does not have such a program, it may seek to bring the foreign employee under one of various umbrella programs, which have already been designated by the United States government. These umbrella programs are sponsored by other organizations who, at the request of the U.S. employer will place a foreign exchange visitor with the sponsor in a United States company. Under some circumstances, the United States company may decide to establish their own exchange-visitor program by filing an application directly with the United States Information Agency. Obviously, this is a time-consuming and expensive step and it would only be feasible under the rarest of circumstances. A small to medium-sized company who did not have experience with foreign exchange visitors in the past might find it difficult to obtain such approval from the United States Information Agency.

The visa is obtained at the U.S. Consulate abroad and the alien must obtain and complete Form IAP-66, Form OF-156, Application for Non-immigrant Visa, give evidence of the foreign person's ability to support him/herself in the U.S.A., proof of his/her intention to depart the United States upon completion of the program, and pay the appropriate fee. The alien must also prove proficiency in the English language.

The J visa holder's family will also receive J-2 visas which will enable them to accompany the J-1 visa holder to the U.S. There is no prohibition against the J-2 visa holder engaging in employment as long as the employment is not for the purpose of providing financial support for the J-1 visa holder.

Requirements. A foreign business trainee must be employed on a full work week basis and must receive compensation equal to at least the prevailing minimum wage and under the prevailing working conditions for the particular industry involved. The purpose of the training must be, of course, to improve the visitor's skills for use in the visitor's home country. Consequently, the alien must maintain a foreign residence which he has no intention of abandoning. Any indication by the foreign exchange visitor that he may be harboring an intention to remain in the United States on a permanent basis may cause the visa to be denied to him.

Two-Year Waiting Period. One of the most unusual characteristics of this visa category is that the foreign exchange visitor will be barred from filing a permanent visa petition or from applying for a change of status to foreign H or L visa for a period of two calendar years from the date of completion of his U.S. training. This rule is applicable to those exchange visitors whose programs have been financed in whole or in part, either by the United States government or by their own governments, or persons who are nationals of countries that the United States Information Agency has determined require the skills and services of people with alien's special training.

Since the nature and purpose of the J visa is to encourage sponsorship entry of third world persons to the United States, neither the United States nor the home country would want the foreign exchange visitor to remain in the United States at the completion of the training program. This would be self-defeating with respect to the program and probably make poor politics between the United States and the alien's home country. Nonetheless, there are procedures to waive the two-year foreign residency requirement, but they are not liberally granted.

While the nature of the waiver application process is beyond the scope of this book, it is possible to highlight the general four conditions which apply. They are as follows:

1. A waiver may be requested by a United States governmental agency on behalf of the exchange alien. This is usually couched in terms of being beneficial to the United States security interest or to that of the public good. Obviously, these situations are somewhat rare.

2. A waiver may be obtained when the foreign residence requirement would result in exceptional hardship to the U.S. citizen or permanent resident, spouse, or child. "Exceptional hardship" is very often difficult to establish in advance, and generally requires intervention of legal counsel. Thus, where a United States citizen marries a foreign exchange visitor while that person is in the United States, it would be very difficult to justify extreme hardship since the U.S. citizen voluntarily embraced the situation. In any event, legal assistance is generally required to properly present an extreme hardship.

3. Another ground for obtaining a waiver of the two-year foreign residency requirement is on the basis of a "no-objection" letter issued by the alien's government to the United States Information Agency stating that the foreign government has "no objection" to the alien remaining in the United States. The United States government is not bound by this no-objection letter, and of course if the United States government will be paying all or a substantial portion of the foreign exchange visitor's costs, then such a letter would have little weight. In any event, these no-objection letters are unavailable to foreign medical graduates.

4. If the alien can prove that he would be subject to persecution in his home country on the basis of race, religion, political opinion, nationality, or membership in a particular social group, then the two year waiting period may also be waived. Proof of possible persecution should be conducted along the same line as a request for political asylum.

The Application Process. The most practical method of bringing an exchange alien into the United States is under an established umbrella program. The sponsoring agency who has already been designated by the United States Information Agency will issue a certificate of eligibility for the exchange visitor status (Form IAP-66) directly to the foreign national and will help arrange the transfer of the alien to the United States for practical training. The J visa holder upon arrival at the border, must present a passport with a valid J visa stamped in it together with Form IAP-66.

3.11 - THE Q VISA - This is a new visa category which permits entry of a person into the United States for purposes of participating in a program designed to provide practical training or employment and the sharing of the history, culture and traditions of the alien's home country. This exchange program will be administered by the Immigration & Naturalization Service instead of the United States Information Agency. The visa is valid for a period of fifteen months and may be applied for at either the U.S. consulate in the alien's home country or in the United States by way of an application for Change of Status. Final administrative regulations will establish the detailed requirements for the petition.

3.12 - THE K VISA.- This visa is issued by the U.S. Consulate abroad to the fiance of a United States Citizen. It is a temporary visa which requires that the foreign person and the U.S. citizen be married within ninety days of entry into the United States. The visa presumes that upon the celebration of the marriage the foreign person will then apply for a permanent visa to the United States and will adjust his/her status in the United States.

The essential requirements are that the parties must establish that they have physically met within the last two years and are actually intent on getting married. In the case of those persons whose religious principles prohibit their meeting before the wedding, the Department of State has relaxed the requirement of a physical meeting, but requires proof of the parties membership in the religion which in fact prohibits the physical meeting prior to the marriage. The proofs required in order to substantiate the physical meeting know of no limitation. In cases that I have handled, I have offered photographs taken of the parties together in myriads of circumstances, including birthday celebrations, other weddings involving other parties, even a ribald photograph or two taken while the parties were celebrating in a nightclub. The U.S. Consular officers are not squeamish, but are rather strict in requiring satisfaction of the statutory and or regulatory requirements.

The U.S. citizen is the Petitioner and must establish that he is a U.S. citizen. Both parties must establish that they are otherwise free to contract marriage. Thus, if either party has been married before, proof of the termination of the previous marriage must be submitted.

If the foreign person marries a person other than the original Petitioner, he/she will be precluded from adjusting status to permanent residency in the United States. Rather, upon approval of a form I-130 from the U.S. citizen or permanent resident spouse, the beneficiary will have to travel abroad to have the visa issued by the U.S. consulate abroad.

In any event, the beneficiary is still subject to the two year conditional visa provision as explained in the section concerning permanent residency based upon marriage to a U.S. citizen (Spouse of a U.S. Citizen) on page 33 of this book.

3.13 THE R VISA - This non-immigrant visa category closely follows the immigrant visa category for special immigrant religious workers. The immigrant religious worker category expires on October 1, 1994, but the R visa category will continue to apply indefinitely.

The principal difference between the immigrant religious worker visa and the R non-immigrant visa is that the R visa category has a five year limitation.

The State Department has recently issued a cable to all diplomatic and consular posts which establishes the guidelines for adjudication of this visa. Parts of the cable are reproduced below since the philosophy of the State Department as to the R non-immigrant visa will also be useful in determining eligibility for the immigrant visa category of religious worker--until October 1, 1994. The cable itself was reproduced in 69 Interpreter Releases 412 (April 6, 1992 edition).

"...There is no requirement in the INA [Immigration & Nationality Act] that applicants for R status establish that they have a residence in a foreign country which they have no intention of abandoning. The (IMMACT90) limits R nonimmigrants to a total period of stay not to exceed five years. The alien's stated intention to depart the United States when his or her status ends is normally sufficient to satisfy (IMMACT90), absent specific indications or evidence that the alien's intent is to the contrary.

Consular Officer is Responsible for Adjudicating R Nonimmigrant Visas

By not madating a preliminary petition process for R nonimmigrants, Congress placed responsibility and authority with consular officers to determine whether the requirements of (IMMACT90) are met for aliens seeking that classification. Consular officers shall process R visa applications in light of these regulations and notes, requesting advisory opinions from the Department when deemed necessary or required per (this cable).

The criteria for classification of an R religious worker are:

(1) The alien is a member of a religious denomination having a bona fide nonprofit, religious organization in the United States;

(2) The religious denomination and its affiliate, if applicable, are exempt from taxation, or the religious denomination qualifies for tax-exempt status;

(3) The alien has been a member of the organization for two years immediately preceding admission;

(4) The alien is entering the United States solely to carry on the vocation of a minister of that denomination; or

(5) At the request of the organization, the alien is entering the United States to work in a religious vocation or occupation for that denomination or for an organization affiliated with the denomination, whether in a professional capacity or not; or

(6) The alien is the spouse or child of an R-1 nonimmigrant who is accompanying or following to join him or her; and

(7) The alien has resided and been physically present outside the United States for the immediate prior year, except for brief visits for business or pleasure, if he or she has previously spent five years in this classification.

Characteristics of a Religious Denomination

A religious denomination will generally be found to have the following elements or comparable indications of its bona fides:

(1) some form of ecclesiastical government;
(2) a recognized creed and form of worship;
(3) a formal code of doctrine and discipline;
(4) religious services and ceremonies;
(5) established places of religious worship; and
(6) religious congregations.

Requirements for a Nonprofit Organization

A bona fide nonprofit organization, as described in...the Internal Revenue Code of 1986, must meet the following criteria:

(1) No part of the net earnings of the organization may benefit any private shareholder or individual;

(2) No substantial part of the organization's activities may involve carrying on propaganda or otherwise attempting to influence legislation; and

(3) The organization may not participate or intervene in any political campaign, including publishing or distributing statements, on behalf of (or opposition to) any candidate for public office.

Membership

The alien must establish that he or she has been a member of the qualifying organization for at least two years immediately preceding application for a visa or for admission. Unlike an applicant for a special immigrant visa as a religious worker, an applicant for R nonimmigrant classification needs only to have been a member of the organization for the required two-year period and needs not to have been engaging in qualifying ministerial, vocational, or occupational activities in addition to membership.

Ministers of Religion

Only individuals authorized by a recognized religious denomination to conduct religious worship and to perform other duties usually performed by authorized members of the clergy of that religion may be classified as ministers of religion. The term does not include lay preachers or other persons not authorized to perform such duties. In all cases, there must be reasonable connection between the activities performed and the religious calling of a minister. Evidence that a person qualifies as a minister or religion is normally available in the form of official ecclesiastical recognition such as certificates of ordination, licenses, formal letters of conferral, etc.

Ordination of Ministers

Ordination of ministers chiefly involves the investment of the individual with ministerial or sacerdotal functions, or the conferral of holy orders upon the individual. If the religious denomination does not have formal ordination procedures, other evidence must be presented to show that the individual has authorization to conduct religious worship and perform other services usually performed by members of the clergy.

A deacon of any recognized religious denomination may be considered to be a minister of religion. Practitioners and nurses of the Christian Science Church ...Commissioned officers of the Salvation Army are considered to be ministers of religion.

Buddhist Monks

The ceremony conferring monkhood status in the Buddhist religion is generally recognized as the equivalent of ordination. Whether or not a Buddhist monk qualifies as a minister of religion...depends upon the activities he is seeking to pursue in the United States...In order to qualify for R status, however, a Buddhist monk must both establish his own qualifications as a minister of religion, and must demonstrate that he is seeking to enter the United States for the sole purpose of conducting religious worship and providing other traditional religious services.

Evidence Forming the Basis for R Classification

An alien seeking classification as a religious worker makes application directly to a consular officer, or, if visa exempt, to an immigration officer at a U.S. port of entry. No petition, labor certification, or prior approval is required. The alien shall present evidence which establishes to the satisfaction of the consular or immigration officer that he or she will be providing services to a bona fide nonprofit, religious organization or its affiliate, and that he or she meets the criteria to perform such services. The evidence to be presented shall consist of the documentation specified below. The alien shall present evidence that the religious denomination, or its affiliate, qualifies as a nonprofit religious organization in the form of:

(1) a certificate of tax-exempt status issued by the Internal Revenue Service; or

(2) in the case of a religious denomination which has never sought tax-exempt status, documentation demonstrating that the organization would qualify for tax exemption...if such status were sought. In all cases involving claimed eligibility for tax exemption, the consular officer must forward all pertinent documentation, along with an evaluation of the evidence presented, to the Department for an advisory opinion.

Certification from Employing Religious Organization

An authorized official of the specific organizational unit of the religious denomination or affiliate which will be employing or engaging the alien in the United States must prepare a letter certifying the following:

(1) that, if the alien's religious membership was maintained, in whole or in part, outside the United States, the foreign and United States religious organizations belong to the same religious denomination;

(2) that, immediately prior to the application for the nonimmigrant visa or application for admission to the United States, the alien has been a member of the religious organization for the required two-year period;

(3) that (as appropriate):

(A) if the alien is a minister, he or she is authorized to conduct religious worship for that denomination and to perform other duties usually performed by authorized members of the clergy of that denomination. The duties to be performed should be described in detail; or

(B) if the alien is a religious professional, he or she has at least a United States baccalaureate degree or its foreign equivalent, that such a degree is required for entry in to the religious profession; or

(C) if the alien is to work in a nonprofessional religious vocation or occupation, he or she is qualified in that vocation or occupation. Evidence of such qualifications may include, but need not be limited to, evidence establishing that the alien is a monk, nun, or religious brother or sister, or that the type of work to be done relates to a traditional religious function;

(4) the arrangements made for remuneration for services to be rendered by the alien, if any, including the amount and source of any salary, a description of any other types of compensation to be received (including housing, food, clothing, and any other benefits to which a monetary value may be affixed), and a statement whether such remuneration shall be in exchange for services rendered.

(5) the name and location of the specific organizational unit of the religious denomination or affiliate for which the alien will be providing services within the United States; and

(6) if the alien is to work for a bona fide organization which is affiliated with a religious denomination, a description of the nature of the relationship between the affiliate and the religious denomination.

A consular officer may request any appropriate additional evidence which is necessary to verify the qualifications of the religious denomination, the alien, or the affiliated organization.

Aliens in R-2 status [spouses and dependents of the R alien] are not authorized to accept employment. The consular officer shall take this into account in evaluating whether family members have furnished adequate evidence of their support while in the United States. R-2 nonimmigrants are permitted to study during their stay in the United States.

R visa recipients should...have all qualifying documentation available when applying for admission, in the event that it is requested by an INS officer at the port of entry.

Length of Stay

The initial period of admission for an R nonimmigrant may not exceed three years. To extend a religious worker's stay, the organizational unit of the religious denomination or affiliate must file Form I-129, petition for nonimmigrant worker, at the INS Service Center having jurisdiction over the place of employment, along with a letter from an authorized official of the organizational unit confirming the worker's continuing eligibility for R classification. An extension may be authorized for a period of up to two years. The religious worker's total period of stay may not exceed five years."

SECTION IV

STRATEGIC PLANNING FOR INBOUND INVESTMENTS

It is important that an investor or other business visitor to the United States (for brevity, we will designate all such persons "investors" in this chapter) understand some pertinent business customs and practices in this country. This section will provide some ideas and examples which may be helpful to investors who may be contemplating a first business visit to the United States for the purpose of completing a transaction that will have certain visa consequences.

If I had to characterize a society with a single concept, then I would characterize the United States as the information society. We are a nation driven by the need to record statistics and data on almost any economic activity of note. While it is sometimes difficult for the lay person to discover the correct information he needs, it is almost always possible to find someone who provides a service for the discovery, compilation and analysis of that information. This wealth of access to information is one of the primary advantages of investing in the United States. Information is almost always available to analyze and accomplish the investment or transaction in a proper and professional manner. Nonetheless, many foreign persons in the United States do not take advantage of these facilities and very often encounter unnecessary problems in the development and execution of their plans.

If an investor wishes to develop an enterprise in a particular location in the United States, he merely has to ask for the critical information and it is usually obtainable. If it is not obtainable, then that in of itself is a relevant finding. Here are some examples:

In the United States almost every state has an economic development agency or industrial promotion board or some other similar bureaucracy whose function it is to stimulate investment and economic growth in that state. These agencies will gladly provide a wealth of information and statistics, free of charge, to anyone inquiring. It is very wise to spend some time corresponding and obtaining information from these sources on the demographic and economic trends within the state, the state's employment policies and the existing labor market. These agencies may also provide information as to the entities and professionals who may be of assistance in a particular field of endeavor. In addition to state governmental programs, there are also local and regional chambers of commerce and related organizations, all of which may be very helpful. The best way to approach the chambers of commerce is to already have a particular plan or scheme in mind and then discuss this with the key person of that body. The local chamber of commerce can be very helpful in pointing out local trends and in making recommendations of banks and other professional services which can be of assistance. The local chamber of commerce also will have much statistical and economic data which can be helpful in further analyzing one's plans. It is often very good to compare any data or other demographic information obtained from the state with the local chamber of commerce and to explore any discrepancies between the two of them.

One should not overlook other sources of information which may be obtained from local or regional trade or industry associations which are easily identifiable through industry and trade journals. These organizations will also have statistical and economic data which will be much more specific to an industry and which will enable one to compare conditions as portrayed on a general basis from the local chambers of commerce or otherwise with the information otherwise obtained from the trade or industry association.

4.1 - The Legal System

The system of law in the United States is probably very different from that with which most foreign persons are familiar. Our system of law evolved from the Common Law of England with its emphasis on the rule of precedent and the lack of a rigid (and predictable) code of law. Parties in a business environment are basically free to establish for themselves the benefits and responsibilities of their transaction or their business relationship. Consequently, the law as it applies to any specific situation may be difficult to discover, thus, the proliferation of lawyers, both general practitioners and specialists. While it is clearly beyond the scope of this book to engage in a general discussion of all the attributes of the legal system as they would affect the affairs of a foreign person, one point needs to be made very clearly. Most states in the United States have laws, judicial precedents and customs which give preference to the words of a contract as opposed to the oral understanding of the parties. This is especially true with respect to the acquisition of real estate, business opportunities, and other types of commercial investments. Thus, the written instrument is given great weight in any dispute by two legally capable parties. The foreign person must be careful that he clearly knows and understands the consequences of any documents that he signs because he/she will be bound to those documents.

4.2 - Real Estate Brokers, Business Brokers, Agents In General

One of the benefits of seeking to invest in the United States is that there is virtually no field or endeavor for which one cannot find a person or entity willing to provide a consulting service. This is the case with respect to the acquisition of land, buildings, shopping centers and business opportunities. There are persons known as real estate brokers who are trained and licensed in each state, and who are presumably expert in the selling and purchasing of real estate of all types, including residential and commercial properties ranging anywhere from the most humble of acquisitions to major urban income producing properties costing hundreds of millions of dollars. A real estate broker can render valuable services to a foreign person by identifying suitable acquisitions within the structure and price range that the foreign investor establishes.

Very often, a long term visa to the United States such as an E-2 or L-1 is only available through the acquisition of an existing U.S. business enterprise. I strongly recommend the use of a business broker in order to find and analyze a suitable business opportunity to acquire, since a business broker is a specialist in the sale and purchase of business opportunities. Most states license and regulate the activities of business brokers and there is at least one national organization which may serve as a referral source to locate a competent business broker in the state of intended residence. That organization is known as the International Business Brokers Association, P.O. Box 247, Concord, Massachusetts 01742 (telephone number: 508-369-5254).

While it is very advisable to use the services of a real estate professional, it is important to understand that in many states a real estate broker, unless special arrangements are made at the beginning of the transaction, represent and work for the seller of the property. This is the case even though the real estate broker may never have met the owner of the property he is selling. In the United States, real estate listing services are often utilized by real estate professionals in order to maximize the number of properties ("listings") that are on the market. In this system a broker who obtains authorization to sell a property ("listing") for a person will record that property in a central listing index called a multiple listing file or multiple property list file, or some other such designation. This list will then be circulated to other real estate professionals who can read a description of the property being sold together with the price and terms, etc. When these other real estate brokers find a prospective buyer who may be interested in purchasing property with those characteristics, they will present the compatible properties from their multiple listing sources to the prospect.

The industry custom, however, is that the seller will pay a commission to whomever sells his property and the "selling" broker is usually a sub-agent of the "listing" broker. The commission is usually divided by the listing broker, that is the broker who listed the property, and the selling broker, the broker that actually procures the buyer. Thus, even though the selling broker may have a personal relationship with the buyer, he actually represents the seller, who, as indicated previously, may be personally unknown to him. The broker's legal and ethical duty is to protect the interest of the seller and obtain for that seller the highest price under the most favorable terms possible.

The system described above, obviously, is not always the best manner for the foreign buyer to approach the purchase of a real estate acquisition in the United States. Since the foreign person does not normally understand the dynamics or the customs of the local market he is usually at a great disadvantage compared to local persons and may not be in a position to derive the best bargain possible. For these reasons, it is strongly recommended that a foreign person acquiring real property and business enterprises in the United States utilize a real estate agent who is committed to representing the buyer only, i.e., a buyer's broker. In this manner, the foreign buyer will derive the most benefit from the experience and skill of the real estate professional. Normally the foreign person will agree to pay the buyer's broker an agreed upon fee or commission, but this in no way involves a price disadvantage as he should be able to reduce the price to the seller by the amount of the commission he is paying his own agent. Again, knowing how this system works enables one to adapt the situation to his best advantage.

If a real estate broker states that even though being paid by and contracted to the seller, he/she will protect the buyer's (foreign investor) interest, the foreign buyer should be forewarned of a potential conflict of interest and should proceed with caution. If the seller acknowledges and accepts this arrangement however, it is usually permissible, though not recommended. The laws of most states do not permit a professional to represent both sides to a transaction. This is a matter of local law and custom that must be determined on a state by state basis and it is the prospective buyer's responsibility to do so.

The concept of "real property" includes raw land, apartment buildings, shopping centers, warehouses and even hotels and motels. Closely related to real estate brokerage (and licensed in the same manner in many states) are business brokers. These are people who specialize in the acquisition and sale of commercial business enterprises which may or may not have any real estate as part of their assets.

Additionally, there are international networks of real estate brokers who specialize in international real estate transactions. One is an organization known by the acronym **FIABCI**, which stands for International Real Estate Federation in the French language. The organization is composed of real estate professionals who specialize in representing foreign purchasers (and sellers) and are experienced in dealing with the needs of foreign persons. The National Association of Realtors also has an international operations section in Washington, D.C. which is composed of U.S. Realtors who have a special interest in international transactions. There probably are **FIABCI** members or other real estate professionals in one's own country who can serve as a referral source to a local U.S. real estate professional who is experienced with the needs of foreign persons.

If one is interested in acquiring or developing a hotel or motel in the United States, one can also contact an organization known as the Hotel and Motel Brokers of America, which is headquartered in Kansas City, Missouri (telephone number 816-891-7070) and whose members are specialists in the acquisition and sale of hotel and motel properties in the United States. The acquisition of a hotel or a large motel, especially one that has other enterprises within it such as a restaurant and/or sports facilities, etc., is generally a good investment for a foreign buyer. This business combines the security of United States real estate with the growth potential of an entrepreneurial enterprise and can qualify an individual to obtain an E visa.

There are many other well qualified real estate professionals in other organizations who may also be of service to a foreign buyer, but it is important to remember the key consideration, and that is to insure that the real estate professional is working as a buyer's agent. I recommend that the "first time" prospective foreign buyer find an honest and competent real estate professional and then work with that person or organization exclusively.

4.3 - LAWYERS

Much has been written and discussed about the proliferation of lawyers in the United States, most of said literature being negative. While it is true that the United States does have many more lawyers per capita than other countries, it is important to remember that the attorney handles many of the functions which, in other countries, are dealt with by notaries and other judicial and quasi-judicial officers. In addition, U.S. law is based on the common law of England which is a jurisprudence molded by judicial precedent rather than by a detailed code. One should also bear in mind that the United States, whether as a result or a cause of the preceding, is a very complex society and has a myriad of business and legal rules which cannot be mastered by a single individual. In addition, it must also be remembered that the laws of each state may vary amongst each other and with the laws of the Federal Government. It is also possible that both federal and state laws may deal with the same subject matter.

It is money well spent to consult with a competent attorney who is experienced or sensitive in dealing with foreign buyers before any purchase transaction is consummated. Such consultation can very often be extremely illuminating and can ensure that the transaction is structured in the most favorable terms for the foreign person. The **American Immigration Lawyers Association** (AILA) is an organization of lawyers in the United States who are experts in the field of Immigration law. Any one interested in obtaining a visa to the United States should only consider dealing with a member of this organization. There are members of this organization in many foreign countries. Also, each state has a Bar Association which can identify lawyers who hold themselves out as experts in a particular field. One can also receive referral advice from other professional persons such as accountants and other types of business and professional consultants.

The foreign investor should, at some point in his negotiations and certainly before any documents are signed, seek professional consultation. The same can also be said for the selection of a qualified accountant and, perhaps, even a consultant versed in the particular field or business of interest to the investor.

One of the most important pieces of information which can be learned from this activity is the glossary of terms applicable to that particular business. There are many business and legal terms that are in use in various jurisdictions of the United States which have no counterpart in a foreign culture. Many terms and customs vary even from state to state or even location to location in the United States. In the real estate field, for example, the use of the terms "escrow agent", "title insurance", "trustee", are all terms that must be clearly understood.

In the United States, the parties are presumed to have read and understood a document which bears their signatures. It is too late after a document has been signed to declare that one had a misconception as to what the document meant or what the meaning was of a particular paragraph. The United States is not a multi-lingual society and very little solace is offered for those who cannot understand the language.

4.4 - TAX PLANNING AND OTHER ECONOMIC CONSIDERATIONS

This section will briefly discuss the various U.S. federal income tax and estate tax consequences as they may affect a foreign person seeking entry into the United States. It is not meant to be a profound or complete analysis of all of the subjects and issues which are pertinent to such an individual, but is merely designed to acquaint a person with important topics. Any foreign person who contemplates an investment in the United States should consult a qualified international tax attorney to advise him of the income and estate tax consequences of the investment. Very often it will be necessary for the U.S. tax attorney to consult with the client's tax and business advisors in his home country in order to ensure complete coverage of all the pertinent issues.

4.5 - GENERAL PRINCIPLES: Residency vs. Non-Residency

The United States is one of the few countries in the world that taxes its citizens and residents on their worldwide income. This very often is a substantial factor to be considered in the overall strategic financial planning by an inbound foreign person. For income tax purposes, there is a profound difference between a citizen or resident of the United States and a "non-resident". These designations may, in fact, have nothing to do with the immigration definition of those terms.

A United States resident, for tax purposes, is any person who is either a U.S. citizen or a person deemed to be a resident of the United States in accordance with the Rules and Regulations of the Internal Revenue Code. A person deemed to be a resident of the United States for tax purposes is anyone who is the holder of a permanent visa to the United States ("green card"). This is sometimes called the "green card" test. This is an absolute test and if a person is a permanent U.S. resident alien, he is automatically and absolutely a resident for income tax purposes under current U.S. law.

In addition to the so-called "green card" test there is also the "substantial presence" test. This test imposes U.S. tax residency on foreign persons who spend a designated time in the United States. These so-called "substantial presence" tests are as follows:

Any person who is present in the United States for thirty-one (31) or more days in the present year is treated as a United States resident if he has also spent 183 more days in the current year or 183 days over a three year period using the following formula.

In the current year, one day of actual presence equals one tax day 1 = 1).

In the previous year, one day of actual presence equals one-third of a day (1 = 1/3).

For the next previous year, one day of actual presence equals one-sixth of a day (1 = 1/6). An example would be helpful. If a person were to reside in the United States for ninety (90) days in 1992, ninety (90) days in 1991, and ninety (90) days in 1990, that person would not be considered a U.S. resident for tax purposes since the total of the above formula does not equal 183 days.

Thus:

1992......90 actual days = 90 equivalent days
1991......90 actual days = 30 equivalent days
1990......90 actual days = 15 equivalent days

TOTAL = 135 days of equivalent presence in the United States under the "substantial presence" test.

In applying the above formula any actual travel days in the United States must also be counted in the equation. For instance, if one enters the United States at 11:30 P.M., that day is considered as a full day in determining the total of days of presence in the United States. Similarly, if one departs the United States at 12:30 A.M. that entire day also is counted in the equation.

There are some specific exemptions that apply to this formula; such as a person who remains in the United States for an extended period because of a medical emergency or who is posted in the United States as a diplomat. There are other exemptions applying to teachers, job trainees and to students. In addition to the above formula, if a person meets the "substantial presence" test under the mathematical computation but can prove that he maintains a home abroad and has closer connections with another jurisdiction, (i.e., he pays taxes in the other jurisdiction), then he may preserve his status as a non U.S. resident for income tax purposes. This possible exception, however, applies only to an individual who has been present in the United States for less than 183 days in the current year.

4.6 - U.S. Income Taxation for Non-Residents

For non-residents, the United States taxes four categories of income, as follows:

1. Income which is effectively connected with a U.S. trade or business. This type of income is taxed on a net taxable income basis, using the normal progressive tax rates otherwise applicable to U.S. taxpayers. Business losses and expenses are allowed to be deducted from gross income in the calculation of net income which is subject to taxation.

2. Income which is known as "Fixed or determinable, annual or periodic income" which is not connected with a U.S. trade or business. This category does not include interest income generated by deposits in qualified U.S. financial institutions such as banks or insurance companies. This latter form of investment interest is not taxable at all.

3. Capital gains income if the foreign person is physically present in the U.S. for more than 183 days in the calendar year. Obviously, if a person is physically present in the United States for more than 183 days in the calendar year he will almost always be deemed to be a U.S. taxpayer.

4. Gain on the sale or other disposition of U.S. real property interests ("USRPI").

Fixed or determinable annual or periodical income is taxed at a flat rate of 30% on the gross amount unless that amount has been reduced by treaty. In addition to the burden of taxation, the tax amount must be withheld at the source of payment by the "withholding agent". This person is usually the last person who has control of the income before it is transferred or conveyed to the foreign person. This type of income is normally considered passive income, such as dividends, interest or royalties, etc.

Thus, it may be in one's financial interest to be considered engaged in a U.S. trade or business if one is receiving rents from real estate investments. Also, there may be a tax treaty in effect between the United States and the foreign person's home country, which may reduce the rate for fixed or determinable annual or periodical income. Additionally, capital gains, that is, the amount of gain realized when a capital asset is sold, associated with the United States property, other than real property, is not taxable as long as the person receiving that income has not been physically present in the United States for 183 or more days. Capital gains on the sale of real property, however, is taxable regardless of the length of time a person has been in the United States.

If the income is from a source outside the United States, then it would not be taxable, unless that income is effectively connected with a U.S. trade or business. There are a number of complex rules that determine the **source** of income and the application and effect of these rules usually requires professional assistance.

4.7 - TAX WITHHOLDING REQUIREMENTS

A primary concern of a foreign person who owns real estate or other income producing assets in the United States is the requirement of withholding a certain percent of the amount of income derived from any asset in the United States for purpose of transmittal to cover tax liability. In order for the withholding rules to apply, the following requirements must exist:

1. There must be a withholding agent. The Internal Revenue Service rules are very broad in defining which persons are required to withhold funds other wise payable to a foreign person. This definition includes real estate brokers, attorneys, other fiduciaries, lessees or mortgagers of real or personal property.

2. The only income which is subject to withholding is, of course, U.S. sources of income.

3. The items which are subject to withholding are fixed determinable and annual or periodic income such as interest, dividends, rent, salaries and other fixed or determinable annual or periodical gains, profit income. Income from the sale of property, real or personal is not considered fixed, determinable, annual or periodic. So capital gains are not subject to withholding unless it involves real estate.

4. The income must not be effectively connected with a U.S. trade or business.

5. The recipient of the income or money must be either a non-resident or alien, foreign partnership or foreign corporation.

6. If there is a treaty or other special rule or exception, then the withholding requirement may be avoided.

7. For partnerships, it should be noted that a domestic partnership is required to withhold and remit to IRS all fixed determinable annual and periodic income (which is not effectively connected with U.S. trader business, which is included in the distributive share of a foreign partner, even if the income is not actually distributed. If the partnership distributive income is effectively connected, then withholding is not required. However, IRS rules and regulations now require a U.S. partnership to withhold and make quarterly estimated tax payments on a foreign partner's share of partnership income which is effectively connected with U.S. trader business regardless of whether distributions of income are actually made to the partners.

8. Trusts, U.S. source, fixed determinable periodic income which is distributed through a trust's foreign beneficiary is subject to withholding.

9. It is extremely important that a foreign person understand that the tax characterization of a business entity by the IRS may determine whether distribution is a dividend and thus taxable by 30% as opposed to any other type of distribution. For example, if a foreign entity is called or designated as a trust or partnership but is in fact a corporation as defined by the IRS, then a distribution may be determined to be a dividend. In the application of treaties, the United States has signed a network of treaties dealing with income tax and withholding requirements with other countries. The primary purpose of the U.S. income tax treaties is the prevention of double taxation. However, some treaties may provide some insular and legitimate tax avoidance opportunities. The advantages offered by U.S. tax treaties have been utilized by corporations formed or otherwise resident in the treaty jurisdiction, controlled by well-advised foreign tax payers whose personal residence is in a country not having a treaty with the U.S., or whose treaty may not be suitable for a particular transaction or investment.

4.8 - GENERAL PLANNING REQUIREMENTS

There are many planning questions which should be answered by a foreign person seeking to make investment in the U.S. prior to that direct investment. Some of them can be characterized as follows:

First of all, the foreign person must determine the priority of his/her objectives with respect to the transfer of assets to the United States. There is always the objective to minimize U.S. and other taxation earnings at the various levels of operation and, of course, to avoid U.S. estate tax. In addition there may be some other very valid immigration objectives which may conflict with some of the above tax concerns, and the foreign person will, of course, make the ultimate decision as to which objective shall be paramount.

Next, some of the questions and issues which need to be considered by a foreign person are as follows:

1. Where will the investor maintain his tax residence?

2. Are there plans in the immediate future or in the near distant future for the investor to relocate?

3. Compare the U.S. tax regimen with the individual and corporate income tax rates and state tax rates in the country of residence or in the country where assets generating income are located.

4. Are there tax treaties available which may change the withholding rules or other U.S. tax requirements otherwise applicable to a non-resident or resident alien.

5. Is the investor making a unique trans-national acquisition in the United States, or is the investor making a plan to generally transfer assets to the U.S.

6. Is the investor already engaged in a business outside of his home country and, if so, where and what are the tax ramifications thereof?

7. Are there other existing U.S. investments, and, if so, are they producing income or loss?

8. Is there need for anonymity on the part of the foreign investor?

9. How will the investment be financed, and by whom?

10. What are the home country laws concerning the repatriation of foreign income earnings for individual residents?

11. What is the anticipated time the investment will be held? Short or long term?

12. What are other relevant business considerations that may affect either the immigration or tax questions?

The tax rates for income "which is effectively connected with a U.S. trade or business" is the same as for residents and is based on a progressive schedule. In addition, the tax is imposed on the net gain of the enterprise. In certain cases a foreign person may elect to be taxed as if he were engaged in a U.S. trade or business. It may be beneficial to be taxed as a U.S. trade or business to avoid the imposition of a tax on the gross income derived from investments in the United States. The rules for this type of election are beyond the scope of this book but it is mentioned here to make the reader aware of the availability of this procedure.

4.9 - NON-RESIDENT ENGAGED IN TRADE OR BUSINESS IN THE UNITED STATES.

If a non-resident alien is engaged in a trade or business in the United States, then all the income effectively connected with that trade or business would be taxable at the same rates and according to the same rules as a United States citizen or resident. There is no clear cut definition of what constitutes a United States trade or business. This determination usually involves a review of the activities of the person and the frequency and nature of those activities. Any business activity that involves significant contacts in the United States or that operates from or in connection with a fixed or permanent office may well cause the taxpayer to be treated as engaged in a trade or business in the United States. Under those circumstances, the income would be taxable.

Various countries have treaties with the United States which provide that the host country will only tax the profits of an enterprise if the alien maintains a "permanent establishment" in that country. There are various definitions of what denotes a "permanent establishment" but it normally includes the maintenance of a business, an office or factory which is in place or is expected to remain in place for a period of twelve months or more. Normally the use of an independent contractor or agent for the representation of a foreign enterprise in the United States will not result in a finding of a permanent establishment unless that independent contractor has wide and general authority to act on behalf of the principal and normally does so.

4.10 - UNITED STATES REAL PROPERTY

A recent amendment to the United States Federal Tax Code known as the Foreign Investment Real Property Tax Act (known as "FIRPTA") essentially places non-resident aliens on an equal footing with United States residents with respect to the tax on the net gains from the sale of United States real property interests. The gain is taxable as if the gain were effectively connected with a United States trade or business. A person is taxable only on the net gain realized in the business and can offset the gross amount realized with expenses, depreciation, etc.

The definition of what is a **real property interest** is quite broad and covers most interests in real property, i.e., land and buildings, except an interest which is purely that of a lender or creditor. Ownership by foreign persons of a hotel and/or motel is, for example, considered ownership of a United States real property interest.

In addition, if a United States corporation owns the United States real property interest, and that interest amounts to at least 50% of the sum of all property owned by that corporation, then it will be considered a United States real property holding corporation and the sale of stock of that corporation will also result in taxation. Payment of the tax is secured by way of a <u>mandatory withholding</u> of 10% of the amount realized on disposition of that United States real property interest. The tax may not equal the 10%, but the withholding agent is required to hold that amount and submit it to the Internal Revenue Service. This is to ensure there will be a fund of money to pay the tax when it is finally determined. The following are exceptions to this withholding requirement:

A. If the property is purchased by a person for use as a residence and the value is $300,000.00 or less, no withholding is required.

B. If the property being sold was not considered an interest in U.S. real property, then the law does not apply; however, according to the law, a U.S. real property interest includes not only real property owned directly by an individual, but also real property owned by a U.S. corporation which, is itself, principally owned by a foreign person. If the property is held by a foreign corporation, and only the shares of stock are sold, then FIRPTA does not apply since the purchaser is only buying shares of stock in a foreign corporation.

C. If the transferred property's corporate stock, which is transferred under an established U.S. securities market, or the transferor has executed and furnished a "non-foreign affidavit" certifying that the transferor is not a foreign person.

Any non-resident alien who was engaged in a trade or business in the United States during the taxable year, or had his income subject to tax by the United States, is required to file an IRS Form 1040NR. There are certain exceptions to this which can be discussed with a tax expert.

Thus, if the United States income tax considerations are important to a foreign investor, the above questions need to be addressed in the pre-immigration planning stages.

4.11 - U.S. ESTATE AND GIFT TAXES

The tax computation for the gross estate of a nonresident alien involves calculations very similar to that of a U.S. person. The following special rules should be born in mind by any foreign person when making an investment in the United States for acquisition of income-producing assets.

1. The situs (that is, the legal location) of real property is determined by its physical location. Thus, real property situated in the United States is considered as having a U.S. situs. Mortgages and liens on real property as a result of loans are not considered as real property for this purpose. They are considered intangible assets.

2. For intangible personal property the situs is also determined by the physical location of the instrument or document which establishes its existence.

3. Stock of a U.S. corporation has its situs in the U.S., whereas stock of a foreign corporation is considered foreign situs regardless of the place of management or location of the stock certificates. As to foreign partnerships, the rule is somewhat unclear. The situs of the partnership is where the partnership business is carried on or managed, not necessarily where the assets are located. What is unclear is whether or not a foreign partnership which is engaged in a U.S. business subjects its entire partnership interest as U.S. situs rather than just its U.S. based situs assets.

4. For currency, situs is its physical location and it is treated just as other tangible personal property.

5. Debt obligation of a U.S. person is considered a U.S. situs property except for the obligation of a U.S. corporation if more than 80% of the gross income of the organization comes from a foreign active source for the three-year prior period.

6. For a sole proprietorship, the physical location of the assets determines their situs.

7. For a grantor trust, property held through a reputable or grantor trust, of which the decedent is the grantor, can be U.S. situs property.

8. Intangible personal property is considered as U.S. situs if it was issued by or enforceable against a resident of the U.S. or domestic corporation or governmental unit.

9. The computation of the tax is identical to that of a U.S. tax payer. There is one exception, and that is that the marital deduction is not allowed the foreign person unless it was granted by treaty or unless the surviving spouse is a U.S. citizen or unless the property is conveyed through a qualified domestic trust. Furthermore, after making the required computations, the rates now range from 18 to 55% of the adjusted estate.

The United States imposes estate taxes on the estate of a non-resident alien if that alien has assets situated in the United States at the time of death. A "non-resident" for purposes of the estate and gift tax laws refers to a person who is not "domiciled" in the United States. "Domicile" is normally defined as the place that a person intends to live permanently, a place that a person has selected as his permanent home. The question of domicile can sometimes be difficult to define precisely. In general, it has been held by the courts that a person can only have one domicile even though he may have many residences. It does not necessarily follow, however, that a person who is domiciled in the United States must be a "resident" for estate tax purposes. Though this result would generally follow, it is technically possible for a person to have a foreign residence (and passport) even though he might be a domiciliary of the United States based upon other considerations and circumstances.

The determination of "residence" for estate tax purposes is of paramount importance to a foreign person in the United States because if he/she is deemed to be a resident then the United States Government may impose an estate tax on the worldwide property held by that person. If the foreign person is considered to be a non-resident alien, then the United States can only impose a federal estate tax on the assets located in the United States at the time of death. The tax rate applicable to a non resident alien is the same as that of a U.S. citizen except that certain of the normal tax credit devices (the marital deduction) are inapplicable. In this situation the **source** rules as to what constitutes U.S. located (situs) property are very important. Currency and other tangible personal property is considered to have a situs based upon physical location. Corporate stock of a U.S. corporation has a U.S. situs while corporate stock of a foreign corporation has a foreign situs, regardless of where the stock certificates are actually located.

Thus, in most situations in which the alien does not intend to reside in the United States for extended periods of time, it is not advisable to hold even residential property or what I consider as "casual property" (condominium apartment, raw land, etc.) in the United States in his or her own name. It is better to have U.S. real property owned by a foreign corporation or a U.S. subsidiary corporation owned by a foreign corporation, since under those circumstances the property will not be deemed to be situated in the United States. Of course, this suggestion must be balanced with the foreign person's other tax interests to ensure that there are no other income tax or other problems created by this device. In general, though, the above is a preferred way of holding property in the United States by a non-resident person. However, before a commitment is made, it is advisable to discuss the tax and other economic consequences of these purchases with a trained professional. This is one of those instances where an hour or two of consultation before taking what may be irrevocable steps can be worth much money and much peace of mind.

4.12 - Investment Reporting Requirements

The federal government has various disclosure laws which provide for the filing of certain reports by a foreign person who owns either agricultural land or other types of business enterprises. The financial threshold for the reporting requirements of commercial business are generally $1,000,000 of cost or of the value of the business assets, as long as there are less than 200 acres of real estate involved.

The Department of Commerce regulations require the reporting of a transaction when a foreign person acquires 10% or more interest in the U.S. business (including real estate). A form BE-13 is filed by a U.S. business within 45 days after the investment. If the foreign person or entity directly acquires a United States real property interest, the form is filed in the name of that foreign person or entity and describes the real property acquired. Form BE-13 identifies each foreign person owning the United States business enterprise and discloses the ultimate beneficial foreign owner, that is, the person or entity in the chain of ownership that is not more that 50% owned by another person, and requests the name, ownership percentage and country of location of each foreign owner. If the ultimate beneficial owner is an individual, however, only the country of residence must be disclosed. Exemptions from filing this form include the acquisition of real estate for personal residence; acquisition of a United States business by U.S. affiliate of a foreign person that merges the U.S. business into its business, if the cost is less than 1 million and less than 200 acres of U.S. land is acquired; an acquisition for establishment of a United States business if its total assets are less than or equal to $1 million and it does not own 200 or more acres of United States land. Bear in mind then the recent provisions for a U.S. investor visa defined in this book. It is clear that upon investment of $1 million which results in the acquisition of a U.S. business, a reporting to the Department of Commerce may be required if the business and its assets includes 200 or more acres of United States land.

These reports are to be used solely for analytical or statistical purposes and are confidential. However, anonymity can never be fully guaranteed. If anonymity is needed, a request for confidentiality can be made in writing to the Department of Commerce. Failure to file the above forms or to provide the information required under these forms may result in civil penalty not exceeding $10,000 or criminal penalty of a fine not exceeding $10,000 or imprisonment up to one year or both. The reporting requirements should not be taken lightly.

The United States Department of Agriculture has a series of reporting requirements for the purpose of monitoring the disposition of agricultural land. Agricultural land is defined as land which currently or within the past five years was used for agricultural, forestry, or timber production purposes unless the land is ten acres or less and the income from the products on the land amounts to less than $1000.00 on an annual basis, or if the land is for personal use. In addition, some states have their own reporting requirements, while other states may have some restrictions on the type of real estate that can be purchased by a non-U.S. resident. All these are factors which should be examined carefully beforehand by a foreign person to ensure that the purchase of certain U.S. assets will be compatible with the investor's overall business plan.

The tax regimen of the United States, as discussed in the previous sections, obviously provides for a considerable amount of disclosure of the foreign person's interest in the United States. In addition to the tax reporting requirements for acquisitions there are also the non-tax reporting requirements under the Department of Agriculture and Department of Commerce rules and regulations mentioned in the previous paragraph.

In addition, there are now reporting requirements known as the EXON-FLORIO regulations which authorize the President of the United States to block or suspend an acquisition by foreign entity of a U.S. business if it negatively affects national security. Administration of this law has been delegated to the Committee of Foreign Investment in the United States (SFIUS). As a result, it is recommended that a foreign person making a transaction that could result in acquisition or control of the U.S. business which may affect U.S. security give notice to the SFIUS. The reason for doing so is to eliminate in a designated time period any future action by the United States to require the foreign investor to divest itself of the investment. The law gives the United States up to three years to issue a divestiture order. Given this, it is certainly worthwhile to give a notice in advance and bring out "into the sunshine" any interest that the United States government may have in the transaction.

A FINAL WORD

When contemplating a transfer of person or property to the United States, the alien should make substantial advanced planning in order to avoid any misunderstandings concerning collateral issues such as income taxation, estate taxation, etc. It is advisable that the investor or executive/manager have a thorough understanding of the philosophy and political theory inherent in the United States immigration system. I cannot over-stress the importance of this pre-entry planning.

This book represents the current law on the topics discussed as of the time of writing. It is not only possible, but probable, that the law will change. I will be pleased to provide updates on the changes in the immigration law to purchasers of this book. In order to receive an update, send me the original page (i) of the Table of Contents of this book, by enclosing it in an envelope with your name and address with the section of law you wish to have updated. I will provide one update to my readers free of charge as soon as possible. In addition, I am available to conduct seminars to private organizations both abroad and in the U.S. on the topics covered in this book, alone or in conjunction with other related presentations. The writer also welcomes any comments and suggestions with respect to the purpose and scope of this book. My office is located in the metropolitan area of Tampa, Florida and my mailing address is as follows:

RAMON CARRION, Attorney at Law
2323 Curlew Road, Suite 7C
Palm Harbor (Clearwater), Florida (U.S.A.) 34683
Telephone: (813) 789-4737

DIRECTORY OF INS OFFICES IN THE UNITED STATES

Following are the addresses of the INS District Offices and Suboffices where papers may be filed. When more than one district is located in a state, you will need to check with one of the offices to determine the correct jurisdiction for filing your papers. Correspondence should be addressed to "Immigration and Naturalization Service, U.S. Department of Justice." **NOTE:** Addresses and telephone numbers may change.

I. NORTHERN REGION
Federal Building
Fort Snelling
Twin Cities, Minnesota 55111
(612) 725-4451

A. Anchorage District
701 C St., Room D229
Anchorage, Alaska 99513
(907) 271-529

1. Fairbanks Suboffice P.O. Box 0208
Fairbanks, Alaska 99706
(907) 474-0307
(Accept papers for filing only)

B. Chicago District
Dirksen Federal Office Bldg.
219 South Dearborn St.
Chicago, Illinois 60604
(312) 353-7334

1. Indiana Suboffice
46 E. Ohio St., Room 124
Indianapolis, Indiana 46204
(317) 269-6009

2. Wisconsin Suboffice
Federal Building
517 E. Wisconsin Ave., Room 186
Milwaukee, Wisconsin 53202
(414) 291-3565

C. Cleveland District
Anthony J. Celebreeze
Federal Building
1240 E. 9th St., Room 1917
Cleveland, Ohio 44199
(216) 522-4770

1. Cincinnati Suboffice
J.W. Peck Federal Bldg.
550 Main St., Room 8525
Cincinnati, Ohio 45202
(513) 684-3781

D. Denver District
1787 Federal Office Bldg.
1961 Stout St.
Denver, Colorado 80294
(303) 844-3526

1. Utah Suboffice
230 W. 400 South St.
Salt Lake City, Utah 84101
(801) 524-5690

E. Detroit District
Federal Building
333 Mt. Elliot St.
Detroit, Michigan 48207
(313) 226-3290

F. Helena District
Federal Building
301 South Park, Room 512
Drawer 10036
Helena, Montana 59626
(406) 449-5288

1. Idaho Suboffice
4620 Overland Road
Boise, Idaho 83705
(208) 334-1821

G. Kansas City District
9747 Conant Avenue
Kansas City, Missouri 64153
(816) 891-0603

1. St. Louis Suboffice
210 N. Tucker Blvd., Room 100
St. Louis, Missouri 63101
(314) 425-4532

H. Omaha District
Federal Office Building
106 S. 15th St., Room 1008
Omaha, Nebraska 68102
(402) 221-4651

I. Portland District
Federal Office Building
511 N.W. Broadway
Portland, Oregon 97209
(503) 221-2271

J. St. Paul District
927 New Post Office Building
180 E. Kellogg Blvd.
St. Paul, Minnesota 55101
(612) 725-7107

K. Seattle District
815 Airport Way South
Seattle, Washington 98134
(206) 442-5959

1. Spokane Suboffice
691 U.S. Courthouse Bldg.
W. 920 Riverside
Spokane, Washington 99201
(509) 456-3824

II. Eastern Region
Federal Building
Elmwood Avenue
Burlington, Vermont 05401
(802) 951-6254

A. Baltimore District
E.A. Garmatz Federal Building
101 W. Lombard St.
Baltimore, Maryland 21201
(301) 962-2120

B. Boston District
John F. Kennedy
Federal Building Room E-132
Government Center
Boston, Massachusetts 02203
(617) 565-3077

1. Connecticut Suboffice
3060 Ribicoff Federal Bldg.
450 Main St.
Hartford, Connecticut 06103
(203) 249-4222

2. Rhode Island Suboffice
Federal Building
Kennedy Plaza, Room 203
Providence, RI 02903
(401) 528-5315

C. Buffalo District
68 Court St.
Buffalo, New York 14202
(716) 846-47312

1. Albany Suboffice
Post Office Building
445 Broadway, Room 227
Albany, New York 12207

D. Newark District
Federal Building
970 Broad St.
Newark, New Jersey 07102
(201) 344-2005

E. New York District
26 Federal Plaza
New York, New York 10278
(212) 206-6500

F. Philadelphia District
U.S. Courthouse
Independence Mall West
601 Market St., Room 1321
Philadelphia, Pennsylvania 19106
(215) 597-7333

1. Pittsburgh Suboffice
2130 Federal Building
1000 Liberty Avenue
Pittsburgh, PA 15222
(412) 644-3356

G. Portland District
76 Pearl St.
Portland, Maine 04112
(207) 780-3352

1. Vermont Suboffice
Federal Building
P.O. Box 328
St. Albans, VT 05478
(802) 524-6743

H. San Juan District
Federal Building
Chardon St., Room 170
Hato Rey, Puerto Rico 00936
(809) 753-4280

1. St. Croix Suboffice
P.O. Box 1270
Kingshill
Christian Sted, St. Croix
Virgin Island 00856
(809) 772-3500

2. St. Thomas Suboffice
Federal Building
P.O. Box 610
Charlotte Amalie,
St. Thomas,
Virgin Islands 00856

I. Washington D.C. District
4420 N. Fairfax Drive
Arlington, Virginia 22203
(703) 235-4055

1. Virginia Suboffice
Norfolk Federal Bldg.
200 Granby Mall
Room 439
Norfolk, VA 23510
(804) 441-3081

III. Southern Region
First International Bldg.
1201 Elm Street, Room 2300
Dallas, Texas 75270
(214) 767-6024

A. Atlanta District
Richard B. Russell
Federal Bldg.
75 Spring St., S.W., Room 1408
Atlanta, Georgia 30303
(404) 221-5158

1. North Carolina Suboffice
6 Woodlawn Green, Room 138
Charlotte, NC 28210
(704) 523-1704

2. South Carolina Suboffice
Federal Building
334 Meeting Street, Room 110
Charleston, SC 29403
(803) 724-4350

B. Dallas District
Federal Building
1100 Commerce Street, Room 6 A21
Dallas, Texas 75242
(214) 767-0514

1. Oklahoma Suboffice
215 Dean A. McGee Ave.
Oklahomas City, OK 73102
(405) 231-4121

C. El Paso District
700 E. San Antonio
P. O. Box 9398
El Paso, Texas 79984
(915) 534-6770

1. New Mexico Suboffice
527 Gold Southwest Ave., Room 1114
Albuquerque, NM 87103
(505) 766-2378

D. Harlingen District
2102 Teege Ave.
Harlingen, Texas 78550
(512) 425-7333

E. Houston District
2627 Caroline
Houston, Texas 77004
(713) 750-1637

F. Miami District
7880 Biscayne Road
Miami, Florida 33138
(305) 536-5741

1. Jacksonville Suboffice
Post Office Building
400 West Bay Street, Room Z-18
P.O. Box 35029
Jacksonville, FL 32210
(904) 791-2624

2. Tampa Suboffice
Federal Building
5509 Gray Street, Room 113
Tampa, Florida 33609
(813) 228-2131

G. New Orleans District
Postal Service Building
701 Loyola Ave., Room T-8005
New Orleans, LA 70113
(504) 589-6533

1. Kentucky Suboffice
U.S. Courthouse Bldg.
W. 6th & Broadway, Room 601
Louisville, KY 40202
(502) 582-6375

2. Tennessee Suboffice
814 Federal Bldg., Room 830
167 N. Main Street
Memphis, TN 38103
(901) 521-3301

H. San Antonio District
U.S. Federal Bldg.
727 E. Durango, Suite A 301
San Antonio, TX 78206
(512) 229-6350

IV. Western Region
Terminal Island
San Pedro, California 90731
(213) 514-6537

A. Honolulu District
595 Ala Moana Blvd.
P.O. Box 461
Honolulu, Hawaii 96813
(808) 541-1379

1. Guam Suboffice
801 Pacific News Bldg.
238 O'Hara Street
P.O. Box DX
Agana, Guam 96910
(671) 472-6411

B. Los Angeles District
300 N. Los Angeles St., Room 1000
Los Angeles, California 90012
(213) 894-2119

C. Phoenix District
Federal Building
230 N. First Ave.
Phoenix, Arizona 85025
(602) 261-3122

1. Tucson Suboffice
Federal Building
300 W. Congress, Rm 8-M
Tucson, Arizona 85701
(602) 629-6228

2. Las Vegas Suboffice
Federal Building
U.S. Courthouse, Room 104
300 Las Vegas Blvd. South
Las Vegas, NV 89101
(702) 388-6251

3. Reno Suboffice
712 Mill Street
Reno, Nevada 89502
(702) 784-5427

D. San Diego District
880 Front Street, Room 1-513
San Diego, California 92188
(619) 233-7036

E. San Francisco District
Appraisers Building
630 Sansome Street
San Francisco, CA 94111
(415) 495-6667

1. Fresno Suboffice
U.S. Courthouse
Federal Building
1130 "O" Street, Room 1308
Fresno, California 93721
(209) 487-5091

2. Sacramento Suboffice
650 Capitol Mall
Sacramento, Calif. 95814
(916) 551-2785

3. San Jose Suboffice
280 S. First Street
San Jose, California 95113
(408) 292-6624

V. Overseas Offices

A. Bangkok District
c/o U.S. Embassy
APO San Francisco, CA 96346

1. Hong Kong Suboffice
c/o Amer. Consulate General
Box 30
FPO San Francisco, CA 96659

2. Manilla Suboffice
c/o American Embassy
1201 Roxas Blvd.
APO San Francisco, CA 96528

3. Seoul Suboffice
c/o American Embassy
APO San Francisco, CA 96301

4. Singapore Suboffice
c/o American Embassy
FPO San Francisco, CA 96699

B. Mexico City District
c/o U.S. Embassy
P.O. Box 3087
Laredo, Texas 78041

1. Guadalajara Suboffice
c/o Amer. Consulate General
P.O. Box 3088
Laredo, Texas 78044

2. Monterrey Suboffice
c/o Amer. Consulate General
P.O. Box 3098
Loredo, Texas 78044

3. Panama City Suboffice
c/o U.S. Embassy
APO Miami, Florida 34002

C. Rome District
c/o U.S. Embassy
APO New York, N.Y. 09794

1. Athens Suboffice
c/o U.S. Embassy
APO New York, N.Y. 09253

2. Frankfurt Suboffice
c/o Amer. Consulate General
Box 12
APO New York, N.Y. 09213

NOTE: The INS has recently opened
an office in New Delhi, India, while
closing its office in Naples, Italy.

The following states have no INS office. The states come under the jurisdiction of the district listed with the state. You must check with that district to see whether the state is serviced by a suboffice within the district.

Alabama (Atlanta)
Arkansas (New Orleans
Delaware (Philadelphia)
Iowa (Omaha)
Kansas (Kansas City)
Mississippi (New Orleans)
New Hampshire (Boston)
North Dakota (St. Paul)
South Dakota (St. Paul)
West Virginia (Philadelphia)
Wyoming (Denver)

NOTE: In addition to the regional and district offices, the INS maintains Regional Service Centers in each region, where many of the routine petitions and applications are sent for adjudication.
The addresses for these centers are:

Eastern Regional Service Center
52 South Main Street
St. Albans, Vermont 05478

Northern Regional Service Center
Federal Building & Courthouse
Room 393
100 Centennial Mall North
Lincoln, Nebraska 68508

Southern Regional Service Center
P.O. Box 152122, Department A
Irving, Texas 75015-2122

Western Regional Service Center
728 East San Ysidro Blvd.
San Ysidro, California 92073

How to File:

A separate application must be filed by each applicant. Applications must be typewritten or clearly printed in ink and completed in full. If extra space is needed to answer any item, attach a continuation sheet and indicate your name, A-number (if any) and the item number.

Note: It is recommended that you retain a complete copy of your application for your records.

Who should file this application?

Certain aliens temporarily in the United States are eligible for employment authorization. Please refer to the ELIGIBILITY SECTION of this application which is found on page three. Carefully review the classes of aliens described in Group A and Group C to determine if you are eligible to apply.

This application should not be filed by lawful permanent resident aliens or by lawful temporary resident aliens.

What is the fee?

Applicants must pay a fee of $35.00 to file this form unless otherwise noted on the reverse of the form. Please refer to page 3. If required, the fee will not be refunded. Pay by cash, check, or money order in the exact amount. All checks and money orders must be payable in U.S. currency in the United States. Make check or money order payable to "Immigration and Naturalization Service." However, if you live in Guam make it payable to "Treasurer, Guam," or if you live in the U.S. Virgin Islands make it payable to "Commissioner of Finance of the Virgin Islands." If the check is not honored the INS will charge you $5.00.

Where should you file this application?

Applications must be presented in person to the nearest Immigration and Naturalization Service (INS) Office that processes employment authorization applications within the jurisdiction over your place of residence. Please bring your INS Form I-94 and any document issued to you by the INS granting you previous employment authorization.

What is our authority for collecting this information?

The authority to require you to file Form I-765, Application for Employment Authorization, is contained in the "Immigration Reform and Control Act of 1986." This information is necessary to determine whether you are eligible for employment authorization and for the preparation of your Employment Authorization Document if you are found eligible. Failure to provide all information as requested may result in the denial or rejection of this application.

The information you provide may also be disclosed to other federal, state, local and foreign law enforcement and regulatory agencies during the course of the investigation required by this Service.

Basic Criteria to Establish Economic Necessity:

Title 45 - Public Welfare, Poverty Guidelines, 45 CFR 1060.2 may be used as the basic criteria to establish eligibility for employment authorization when the applicant's economic necessity is identified as a factor. If you are an applicant who must show economic necessity, you should include a statement listing all of your assets, income, and expenses as evidence of your economic need to work.

Note: Not all applicants are required to establish economic necessity. Carefully review the ELIGIBILITY SECTION of the application. Only aliens who are filing for employment authorization under Group C, items (c)(10), (c)(13), and (c)(14) are required to furnish information on economic need. This information must be furnished on attached sheet(s) and submitted with this application.

What are the penalties for submitting false information?

Title 18, United States Code, Section 1001 states that whoever willfully and knowingly falsifies a material fact, makes a false statement, or makes use of a false document will be fined up to $10,000 or imprisoned up to five years, or both.

Title 18, United States Code, Section 1546(a) states that whoever makes any false statement with respect to a material fact in any document required by the immigration laws or regulations, or presents an application containing any false statement shall be fined or imprisoned or both.

Please Complete Both Sides of Form.

Reporting Burden: Public reporting burden for this collection of information is estimated to average sixty (60) minutes per response, including the time for reviewing instructions, searching existing data sources, gathering and maintaining the data needed, and completing and reviewing the collection of information. Send comments regarding this burden estimate or any other aspect of this collection of information, including suggestions for reducing this burden, to: U.S. Department of Justice, Immigration and Naturalization Service, Room 2011, Washington, D.C. 20536, and to the Office of Management and Budget, Paperwork Reduction Project. OMB No. 1115-0163, Washington, D.C. 20503.

Form I-765 (08/24/89) Page 1

U. S. Department of Justice
Immigration and Naturalization Service

OMB # 1115-0163
Application for Employment Authorization

Do Not Write in This Block

Please Complete Both Sides of Form

Case ID#	Action Stamp	Fee Stamp
A#		
Applicant is filing under 274a.12 _____		Remarks

☐ Application Approved. Employment Authorized / Extended (Circle One) _____ (Date).
   until _____ (Date).

   Subject to the following conditions: _____

☐ Application Denied.
   ☐ Failed to establish eligibility under 8 CFR 274a.12 (a) or (c).
   ☐ Failed to establish economic necessity as required in 8 CFR 274a.12(c), (10), (13), (14).

I am applying for:
☐ Permission to accept employment
☐ Replacement (of lost employment authorization document).
☐ Extension of my permission to accept employment (attach previous employment authorization document).

1. Name (Family Name in CAPS) (First) (Middle)

2. Other Names Used (Include Maiden Name)

3. Address in the United States (Number and Street) (Apt. Number)

   (Town or City) (State/Country) (ZIP Code)

4. Country of Citizenship

5. Place of Birth (Town or City) (State/Province) (Country)

6. Date of Birth (Month/Day/Year) 7. Sex
   ☐ Male ☐ Female

8. Marital Status ☐ Married ☐ Single
   ☐ Widowed ☐ Divorced

9. Social Security Number (Include all Numbers you have ever used)

10. Alien Registration Number (A-Number) or I-94 Number (if any)

11. Have you ever before applied for employment authorization from INS?
    ☐ Yes (If yes, complete below) ☐ No
    Which INS Office? Date(s)

    Results (Granted or Denied - attach all documentation)

12. Date of Last Entry into the U.S. (Month/Day/Year)

13. Place of Last Entry into the U.S.

14. Manner of Last Entry (Visitor, Student, etc.)

15. Current Immigration Status (Visitor, Student, etc.)

16. Go to the Eligibility Section on the reverse of this form and check the box which applies to you. In the space below, place the number of the box you selected on the reverse side:

    Eligibility under 8 CFR 274a.12

    (   ) (   ) (   )

Complete the reverse of this form before signature.

Your Certification: I certify, under penalty of perjury under the laws of the United States of America, that the foregoing is true and correct. Furthermore, I authorize the release of any information which the Immigration and Naturalization Service needs to determine eligibility for the benefit I am seeking. I have read the reverse of this form and have checked the appropriate block, which is identified in item #16, above.

Signature _____ Telephone Number _____ Date _____

Signature of Person Preparing Form if Other Than Above: I declare that this document was prepared by me at the request of the applicant and is based on all information of which I have any knowledge.

Print Name _____ Address _____ Signature _____ Date _____

Initial Receipt	Resubmitted	Relocated		Completed		
		Rec'd	Sent	Approved	Denied	Returned

Form I-765 (08/24/89) Page 2

GROUP A

The current immigration laws and regulations permit certain classes of aliens to work in the United States. If you are an alien described within one of the classes below, you do not need to request that employment authorization be granted to you, but you do need to request a document to show that you are able to work in the United States. **NO FEE will be required for your original card. If you need a replacement employment authorization document the fee will be required to process your request.**

Place an **X** in the box next to the number which applies to you.

☐ (a) (3) - I have been admitted to the United States as a refugee.

☐ (a) (4) - I have been paroled into the United States as a refugee.

☐ (a) (5) - My application for asylum has been granted.

☐ (a) (6) - I am the fiancé(e) of a United States citizen and I have K-1 nonimmigrant status; **OR** I am the dependent of a fiancé(e) of a United States citizen and I have K-2 nonimmigrant status.

☐ (a) (7) - I have N-8 or N-9 nonimmigrant status in the United States.

☐ (a) (8) - I am a citizen of the Federated States of Micronesia or of the Marshall Islands.

☐ (a) (9) - I have been granted suspension of deportation and I have not yet been granted lawful permanent resident status in the United States.

☐ (a) (10) - I have been granted withholding of deportation.

☐ (a) (11) - I have been granted extended voluntary departure by the Attorney General.

GROUP C

The immigration law and regulations allow certain aliens to apply for employment authorization. If you are an alien described in one of the classes below you may request employment authorization from the INS and, if granted, you will receive an employment authorization document.

Place an **X** in the box next to the number which applies to you.

☐ (c) (1) - I am the dependent of a foreign government official (A-1 or A-2). I have attached certification from the Department of State recommending employment. **NO FEE.**

☐ (c) (2) - I am the dependent of an employee of the Coordination Council of North American Affairs and I have E-1 nonimmigrant status. I have attached certification of my status from the American Institute of Taiwan. **FEE REQUIRED.**

☐ (c) (3) (i) - I am a foreign student (F-1). I have attached certification from the designated school official recommending employment for economic necessity. I have also attached my INS Form I-20 ID copy. **FEE REQUIRED.**

☐ (c) (3) (ii) - I am a foreign student (F-1). I have attached certification from the designated school official recommending employment for practical training. I have also attached my INS Form I-20 ID copy. **FEE REQUIRED.**

☐ (c) (3) (iii) - I am a foreign student (F-1). I have attached certification from my designated school official and I have been offered employment under the sponsorship of an international organization within the meaning of the International Organization Immunities Act. I have certification from this sponsor and I have also attached my INS Form I-20 ID copy. **FEE REQUIRED.**

☐ (c) (4) - I am the dependent of an officer or employee of an international organization (G-1 or G-4). I have attached certification from the Department of State recommending employment. **NO FEE.**

☐ (c) (5) - I am the dependent of an exchange visitor and I have J-2 nonimmigrant status. **FEE REQUIRED.**

☐ (c) (6) - I am a vocational foreign student (M-1). I have attached certification from the designated school official recommending employment for practical training. I have also attached my INS Form I-20ID Copy. **FEE REQUIRED.**

☐ (c) (7) - I am the dependent of an individual classified as NATO-1 through NATO-7. **FEE REQUIRED.**

☐ (c) (8) - I have filed an application for asylum in the United States and the application is pending. **FEE REQUIRED FOR REPLACEMENT ONLY.**

☐ (c) (9) - I have filed an application for adjustment of status to lawful permanent resident status and the application is pending. **FEE REQUIRED.**

☐ (c) (10) - I have filed an application for suspension of deportation and the application is still pending. **I understand that I must show economic necessity and I will refer to the instructions concerning "Basic Criteria to Establish Economic Necessity." FEE REQUIRED.**

☐ (c) (11) - I have been paroled into the United States for emergent reasons or for reasons in the public interest. **FEE REQUIRED.**

☐ (c) (12) - I am a deportable alien and I have been granted voluntary departure either prior to or after my hearing before the immigration judge. **FEE REQUIRED.**

☐ (c) (13) - I have been placed in exclusion or deportation proceedings. I have not received a final order of deportation or exclusion and I have not been detained. **I understand that I must show economic necessity and I will refer to the instructions concerning "Basic Criteria to Establish Economic Necessity." FEE REQUIRED.**

☐ (c) (14) - I have been granted deferred action by INS as an act of administrative convenience to the government. **I understand that I must show economic necessity and I will refer to the instructions concerning "Basic Criteria to Establish Economic Necessity." FEE REQUIRED.**

☐ (c) (15) (i) - I am a nonimmigrant temporary worker (H-1, H-2, H-3) and I have filed a timely application for extension of my stay. My application for extension has not been adjudicated within 120 days. **FEE REQUIRED.**

☐ (c) (15) (ii) - I am a nonimmigrant exchange visitor (J-1) and I have filed a timely application for extension of my stay. My application for extension has not been adjudicated within 120 days. **FEE REQUIRED.**

☐ (c) (15) (iii) - I am a nonimmigrant intracompany transferee (L-1) and I have filed a timely application for extension of my stay. My application has not been adjudicated within 120 days. **FEE REQUIRED.**

☐ (c) (15) (iv) - I am a nonimmigrant E-1, E-2, I, A-3, or G-5 and I have filed a timely application for extension of my stay. My application has not been adjudicated within 120 days. **FEE REQUIRED.**

U.S. Department of Justice

Immigration and Naturalization Service

Instructions for Completing

Petition for a Nonimmigrant Worker

Form I-129

Form I-129 (12/11/91)N

Purpose Of This Form.

This form is for an employer to petition for an alien to come to the U.S. temporarily to perform services or labor, or to receive training, as an H-1A, H-1B, H-2A, H-2B, H-3, L-1, O-1, P-2, or Q nonimmigrant worker.

This form is also for an employer to petition for an extension of stay or change of status for an alien as an E-1, E-2, R-1 or TC nonimmigrant. A petition is not required to apply for an E-1, E-2 or R-1 nonimmigrant visa or admission as a TC nonimmigrant. A petition is only required to apply for a change to such status or an extension of stay in such status.

This form consists of a basic petition, and different supplements that apply to each specific classification.

Who May File.
General. A U.S. employer may file to classify an alien in any nonimmigrant classification listed below. A foreign employer may file for certain classifications as indicated in the specific instructions.

Agents. A U.S. individual or company in business as an agent may file for types of workers who are traditionally self-employed or who traditionally use an agent to arrange short-term employment with numerous employers. A petition filed by an agent must include a complete itinerary of services or engagements, including dates, names and addresses of the actual employers, and the locations where the services will be performed. The agent must guarantee the wage offered and the other terms and conditions of employment by contract with the alien(s).

Including more than one alien in a petition. Aliens who will apply for their visas at the same consulate or, if they do not need visas, will enter at the same port of entry may be included in one petition filed by an employer or agent in the following classifications if the dates of employment are the same:
- H-1B if they are members of the same entertainment group or athletic team (accompanying aliens must be filed for on a separate petition);
- H-1B accompanying aliens if they will accompany the same H-1B or same H-1B group of artists, entertainers or athletes for the same period of time, in the same occupation, and in the same location(s);
- H2-A if they are included on the same labor certification and will perform the same duties;
- H-2B if they are included on the same labor certification and will perform the same duties;
- H-3 if they will receive the same training;
- P-2 if they are members of the same group (accompanying aliens must be filed for on a separate petition);
- P-2 accompanying aliens if they will accompany the same P-2 alien or group for the same period of time, in the same occupation, and in the same location(s);
- Q if they will be involved in the same international cultural exchange program.

Multiple locations. A petition for alien(s) to perform services or labor or receive training in more than one location must include an itinerary with the dates and locations where the services or training will take place.

Unnamed aliens. All aliens in a petition for an extension of stay or change of status must be named in the petition. All aliens included in any other petition must be named except:
- an H-2A petition for more than one worker may include unnamed aliens if they are unnamed on the labor certification;
- an H-2B petition for more than one worker may include unnamed aliens in emergent situations where you establish in the petition that you cannot yet provide names due to circumstances which you could not anticipate or control.

Where some or all of the aliens are not named, specify the total number of unnamed aliens and total number of aliens in the petition. Where the aliens must be named, petitions naming subsequent beneficiaries may be filed later with a copy of the same labor certification. Each petition must reference all previously filed petitions using that certification.

General Filing Instructions.

Complete the basic form and relating supplement. Indicate the specific classification you are requesting. Please answer all questions by typing or clearly printing in black ink. Indicate that an item is not applicable with "N/A". If the answer is "none," write "none". If you need extra space to answer any item, attach a sheet of paper with your name and your alien registration number (A#), if any, and indicate the number of the item to which the answer refers. You must file your petition with the required Initial Evidence. The petition must be properly signed and filed with the proper fee. Submit the petition in duplicate if you check block "a" or "b" in question 4 of Part 2 on the form.

Classification; Initial Evidence.

These instructions are divided into two parts. The first looks at classifications which require a petition for an initial visa or entry and for any extension or change of status. The second looks at those classifications which only require a petition for a change of status or extension of stay.

▶ **Petition always required:** The following classifications always require a petition. A petition for new or concurrent employment or for extension where there is a change in previously approved employment must be filed with the initial evidence listed below, and with the initial evidence required by the separate instructions for a change of status or extension of stay. However, a petition for an extension based on unchanged, previously approved employment need only be filed with the initial evidence required in the separate extension of stay instructions.

H-1A. An H-1A is an alien coming to perform services as a registered professional nurse. The petition must be filed by a U.S. employer that provides health care services (including nursing contractors), and must be filed with:

- evidence the alien has a full and unrestricted license to practice professional nursing in the country where he or she obtained nursing education, or that the nursing education was received in the U.S. or Canada;
- evidence the alien has either;
  - passed the test given by the Commission on Graduate of Foreign Nursing Schools (CGFNS),

- a permanent license to practice professional nursing in the state of intended employment, or
- a permanent license to practice professional nursing in any state or territory of the U.S. and has temporary authorization to practice professional nursing in the state of intended employment;
- evidence the alien is fully qualified and eligible under the laws of the state or territory of intended employment to work as a professional nurse immediately after entry;
- a statement indicating you intend to employ the alien solely as a registered professional nurse; and
- a copy of the Department of Labor's current notice of acceptance of the filing of your attestation on Form ETA 9029.

H-1B. An H-1B is an alien coming temporarily to perform services in a specialty occupation. A specialty occupation is one which requires the theoretical and practical application of a body of highly specialized knowledge to fully perform the occupation and requires completion of a specific course of education culminating in a baccalaureate degree in a specific occupational specialty. Write **H-1B1** in the classification requested block. The petition must be filed by the U.S. employer, and must be filed with:

- an approved labor condition application from the Department of Labor;
- evidence the proposed employment qualifies as within a specialty occupation;
- evidence the alien has the required degree by submitting either:
  - a copy of the person's U.S. baccalaureate or higher degree which is required by the specialty occupation,
  - a copy of a foreign degree and evidence it is equivalent to the U.S. degree, or
  - evidence of education and experience which is equivalent to the required U.S. degree;
- a copy of any required license or other official permission to practice the occupation in the state of intended employment; and
- a copy of any written contract between you and the alien or a summary of the terms of the oral agreement under which the alien will be employed.

H1-B. An H-1B is also an alien coming to perform services of an exceptional nature relating to a cooperative research and development project administered by the Department of Defense. A U.S. employer may file the petition. Write **H-1B2** in the classification requested block. It must be filed with:

- a description of the proposed employment and evidence the services and project meet the above conditions; and
- a statement listing the names of all aliens who are not permanent residents who are have been employed on the project within the past year, along with their dates of employment.

H-1B. An H-1B is also an artist, entertainer or fashion model who has national or international acclaim and recognition for achievements, individually or, in the case of entertainers, as part of a group, to be employed in a capacity requiring someone of distinguished merit and ability. (See the separate instructions for accompanying personnel.) A U.S. employer or foreign employer may file the petition. Write **H-1B3** in the classification requested block. It must be filed with:

- copies of evidence the alien or group is nationally or internationally recognized in the discipline by submitting at least 3 different types of documentation showing that the group:
  - has performed and will perform as a starring or leading entertainment group in productions or events which have a distinguished reputation as evidenced by critical reviews, advertisements, publicity releases, publications, or contracts,
  - has achieved national or international recognition and acclaim for outstanding achievement in their field as evidenced by reviews in major newspapers, trade journals, magazines, or other published material,
  - has received significant national or international awards or prizes for outstanding achievement in their field,
  - has performed and will perform services as a leading or starring group for organizations and establishments that have a distinguished reputation,

- has a record of major commercial or critically acclaimed successes, as evidenced by such indicators as ratings, or standing in the field, box office receipts, record, cassette, or video sales, and other achievements in the field as reported in trade journals, major newspapers, or other publications,
- has received significant recognition for achievements from organizations, critics, government agencies or other recognized experts in the field,
- has received significant recognition for achievements from organizations, critics, government agencies or other recognized experts in the field,
- commands a high salary or other substantial remuneration for services, evidenced by contracts or other reliable evidence;
- copies of evidence the services to be performed require a person of distinguished merit and ability and either:
  - involve an event, production or activity which has a distinguished reputation; or
  - the services are as a lead or starring participant in a distinguished activity for an organization or establishment that has a distinguished reputation or record of employing persons of distinguished merit and ability.

H-1B. An H-1B is also an alien coming temporarily to perform as an artist or entertainer, individually or as part of a group, in a unique or traditional art form. (See the separate instructions for accompanying personnel.) A U.S. employer or foreign employer may file the petiion. Write **H-1B4** in the classification requested block. It must be filed with:

- a description of the proposed activities and evidence they constitute a unique or traditional art form;
- affidavits, testimonials or letters from recognized experts attesting to the authenticity and excellence of the skills of the alien or group in presenting the unique or traditional art form and explaining the level of recognition accorded the alien or group in the native country and the U.S.;

- copies of evidence most of the performances or presentations will be culturally unique events sponsored by educational, cultural, or governmental agencies; and
- either:
  - an affidavit or testimonial from the ministry of culture, USIA Cultural Affairs Officer, the academy for the artistic discipline, a leading scholar, a cultural institution, or a major university in the alien's own country or from a third country,
  - a letter from a U.S. expert who has knowledge in the particular field, such as scholar, arts, administrator, critic, or representative of a cultural organization or government agency, or
  - a letter or certification from a U.S. government cultural or arts agency such as the Smithsonian Institution, the National Endowment for the Arts, the National Endowment for the Humanities, or the Library of Congress.

H-1B. An H-1B is also an alien coming temporarily to perform at a specific athletic competition as an athlete, individually or as part of a group or team, at a nationally or internationally recognized level of performance. (See the separate instructions for accompanying personnel.) A U.S. employer or foreign employer may file the petition. Write **H-1B5** in the classification requested block. The petition must be filed with:

- a copy of the contract with a major U.S. sports league or team or contract in an individual sport commensurate with national or international recognition in that sport.
- copies of evidence of at least 2 of the following:
  - participation to a substantial extent in a prior season with a major U.S. sports league,
  - participation in international competition with a national team,
  - participation to a substantial extent in a prior season for a U.S. college or university in intercollegiate competition,
  - a written statement from an official of a major U.S. sports league or an official of the governing body of the sport detailing how the alien or team is nationally orinternationally recognized,

- a written statement from a member of the sports media or a recognized expert in the sport detailing how the alien or team is nationally or internationally recognized,
- the individual or team is ranked if the sport has national or international rankings, or
- the alien or team has received a significant honor or award in the sport.

H-1B Accompanying Support Personnel. Accompanying support personnel are highly skilled aliens coming temporarily as an essential and integral part of the competition or performance of a H-1B artist, entertainer or athlete because they perform support services which cannot be readily performed by a U.S. worker and which are essential to the successful performance or services by the H-1B. The aliens must each also have significant prior work experience with the H-1B alien. Write *H-1BS* in the classification requested block on the petition. The petition must be filed in conjunction with the employment of a H-1B alien. The petition must be filed with:

- a statement describing the alien's prior and current essentiality, critical skills and experience with the H-1B;
- statements or affidavits from persons with first hand knowledge that the alien has had substantial experience performing the critical skills and essential support services for the H-1B; and
- a copy of any written contract between you and the alien or a summary of the terms of the oral agreement under which the alien will be employed.

H-2A. An H-2A is an alien coming temporarily to engage in temporary or seasonal agricultural employment. The petition must be filed by a U.S. employer or an association of U.S. agricultural producers named as a joint employer on the certification. The petition must be filed with:

- a single valid temporary agricultural labor certification, or, if U.S. workers do not appear at the worksite, a copy of the Department of Labor's denial of a certification and appeal, and evidence that qualified domestic labor is unavailable; and
- copies of evidence that each named alien met the minimum job requirements stated in the certification when it was applied for.

H-2B. An H-2B is an alien coming temporarily to engage in non-agricultural employment which is seasonal, intermittent, to meet a peak load need, or for a one-time occurrence. The petition must be filed by a U.S. employer with:

- either:
  - a temporary labor certification from the Department of Labor, or the Governor of Guam if the proposed employment is solely in Guam, indicating that qualified U.S. workers are not available and that employment of the alien will not adversely affect the wages and working conditions of similarly employed U.S. workers, or
  - a notice from such authority that such certification cannot be made, along with evidence of the unavailability of U.S. workers and of the prevailing wage rate for the occupation in the U.S., and evidence overcoming each reason why the certification was not granted; and
- copies of evidence, such as employment letters and training certificates, that each named alien met the minimum job requirements stated in the certification when it was applied for.

H-3. An H-3 is an alien coming temporarily to participate in a special education training program in the education of children with physical, mental, or emotional disabilities. Custodial care of children must be incidental to the training program. The petition must be filed by the U.S. employer with:

- a description of the training, staff and facilities, evidence the program meets the above conditions, and details of the alien's participation in the program; and
- evidence the alien is nearing completion of a baccalaureate degree in special education, or already holds such a degree, or has extensive prior training and experience in teaching children with physical, mental, or emotional disabilities.

H-3. An H-3 is also an alien coming temporarily to receive other training from an employer in any field other than graduate education or training. The petition must be filed by the U.S. employer with:

- a detailed description of the structured training program, including the number of classroom hours per week and the number of hours of on-the-job training per week;
- a summary of the prior training and experience of each alien in the petition; and
- an explanation of why the training is required, whether similar training is available in the alien's country, how the training will benefit the alien in pursuing a career abroad, and why you will incur the cost of providing the training without significant productive labor.

L-1. An L-1 is an alien coming temporarily to perform services in a managerial or executive capacity, for the same corporation or firm, or for the branch, subsidiary or affiliate of the employer which employed him or her abroad for one continuous year within the three-year period immediately preceding the filing of the petition, in an executive, managerial or specialized knowledge capacity. Write **L-1A** in the classification requested block on the petition.

L-1. An L-1 is also an alien coming temporarily to perform services which entail specialized knowledge, for the same corporation or firm, or for the branch, subsidiary or affiliate of the employer which employed him or her abroad for one continuous year within the three year period immediately preceding the filing of the petition, in an executive, managerial or specialized knowledge capacity. Specialized knowledge is special knowledge of the employer's product or its application in international markets or an advanced level of the knowledge of the employer's processes and procedures. Write **L-1B** in the classification requested block on the petition.

L Petition Requirements. A U.S. employer or foreign employer may file the petition, but a foreign employer must have a legal business entity in the U.S. The petition must be filed with:

- evidence of the qualifying relationship between the U.S. and foreign employer based on ownership and control, such as an annual report, articles of incorporation, financial statements or copies of stock certificates;

- a letter from the alien's foreign qualifying employer detailing his/her dates of employment, job duties, qualifications and salary, demonstrating that the alien worked for the employer for at least one continuous year in the three-year period preceding the filing of the petition in an executive, managerial or specialized knowledge capacity; and
- a description of the proposed job duties and qualifications and evidence the proposed employment is in an executive, managerial or specialized knowledge capacity.

If the alien is coming to the U.S. to open a new office, also file the petition with copies of evidence the business entity in the U.S.:
- already has sufficient premises to house the new office;
- has or upon establishment will have the qualifying relationship to the foreign employer;
- has the financial ability to remunerate the alien and to begin doing business in the U.S., including evidence about the size of the U.S. investment, the organizational structure of both firms, the financial size and condition of the foreign employer, and, if the alien is coming as an L-1 manager or executive to open a new office, such evidence must establish that the intended U.S. operation will support the executive or managerial position within one year.

Blanket L petition. An L blanket petition simplifies the process of later filing for individual L-1A workers and L-1B workers who are specialized knowledge professionals, which are persons who possess specialized knowledge employed in positions which require the theoretical and practical application of a body of highly specialized knowledge to fully perform the occupation and require completion of a specific course of education culminating in a baccalaureate degree in a specific occupational specialty.

A blanket L petition must be filed by a U.S. employer who will be the single representative between INS and the qualifying organizations. Write **LZ** in the classification requested block. Do not name an individual employee. File the petition with copies of evidence that:

- you and your branches, subsidiaries and affiliates are engaged in commercial trade or services;
- you have an office in the U.S. that has been doing business for one year or more;
- you have 3 or more domestic and foreign branches, subsidiaries, or affiliates;
- you and your qualifying organizations have obtained approved petitions for at least 10 "L" managers, executives or specialized knowledge professionals during the previous 12 months, have U.S. subsidiaries or affiliates with combined annual sales of at least 25 million dollars, or have a U.S. work force of at least 1,000 employees.

After approval of a blanket petition, you may file for individual employees to enter as an L-1A alien or L-1B specialized knowledge professional under the blanket petition. If the alien is outside the U.S., file Form I-129S. If the alien is already in the U.S., file the I-129 to request a change of status based on this blanket petition. The petition must be filed with:
- a copy of the approval notice for the blanket petition;
- a letter from the alien's foreign qualifying employer detailing his/her dates of employment, job duties, qualifications, and salary for the 3 previous years; and
- if the alien is a specialized knowledge professional, a copy of a U.S. degree, a foreign degree equivalent to a U.S. degree, or evidence establishing the combination of the beneficiary's education and experience is the equivalent of a U.S. degree.

O-1. An O-1 is an alien coming temporarily who has extraordinary ability in the sciences, education or business. A U.S. employer or foreign employer may file the petition. The petition must be filed with:
- a written consultation with a peer group in the alien's area of ability (see GENERAL EVIDENCE);
- a copy of any written contract between you and the alien or a summary of the terms of the oral agreement under which the alien will be employed.
- copies of evidence the services to be performed either:

- primarily involve a specific scientific or educational project, conference, convention, lecture, or exhibit sponsored by scientific or educational organizations or establishments, or
- consist of a specific business project that requires an extraordinary executive, manager, or highly technical person due to the complexity of the project;
- evidence the alien has received a major, internationally-recognized award, such as a Nobel Prize, or copies of evidence of at least three of the following:
  - receipt of nationally or internationally recognized prizes or awards for excellence in the field of endeavor,
  - membership in associations in the field which require outstanding achievements as judged by recognized international experts,
  - published material in professional or major trade publications or newspapers about the alien and his work in the field,
  - participation on a panel or individually as a judge of the work of others in the field or an allied field,
  - original scientific or scholarly research contributions of major significance in the field,
  - authorship of scholarly articles in the field in professional journals or other major media, or
  - evidence the alien commands a high salary or other high remuneration for services.

P-2. A P-2 is an alien coming temporarily to perform as an artist or entertainer, individually or as part of a group, under a reciprocal exchange program between an organization in the U.S. and an organization in another country. (See the separate instructions for accompanying personnel.) The petition must be filed by the sponsoring organization or employer in the U.S. It must be filed with:
- written consultation with an appropriate labor organization (see GENERAL EVIDENCE);

- a copy of the formal reciprocal exchange agreement between the U.S. organization(s) sponsoring the aliens, and the organization(s) in a foreign country which will receive the U.S. artist or entertainers;
- a statement from the sponsoring organization describing the reciprocal exchange, including the name of the receiving organization abroad, names and occupations of U.S. artists or entertainers being sent abroad, length of their stay, activities in which they will be engaged and the terms and conditions of their employment; and
- copies of evidence the aliens and the U.S. artists or entertainers are experienced artists with comparable skills and that the terms and conditions of employment are similar.

P-2 Accompanying Support Personnel. Accompanying support personnel are highly skilled aliens coming temporarily as an essential and integral part of the competition or performance of a P-2, or because they perform support services which cannot be readily performed by a U.S. worker and which are essential to the successful performance or services by the P-2. The aliens must each also have significant prior work experience with the P-2 alien. Write *P-2S* in the classification requested block on the petition. The petition must be filed in conjunction with the employment of a P-2 alien. The petition must be filed with:
- written consultation with a labor organization in the skill in which the alien will be involved (see GENERAL EVIDENCE);
- a statement describing the alien's prior and current essentiality, critical skills and experience with the P-2;
- statements or affidavits from persons with first hand knowledge that the alien has had substantial experience performing the critical skills and essential support services for the P-2, and
- a copy of any written contract between you and the alien or a summary of the terms of the oral agreement under which the alien will be employed.

Q. A Q is an alien coming temporarily to participate in an international cultural exchange program approved by the Attorney General for the sharing of the attitude, customs, history, heritage, philosophy, and/or traditions of the alien's country of nationality. The culture sharing must take place in a school, museum, business, or other establishment where the public is exposed to aspects of a foreign culture as part of a structured program. The work component of the program may not be independent of the cultural component, but must serve as the vehicle to achieve the objectives of the cultural component. A U.S. employer or foreign employer may file the petition; however, a foreign employer's petition must be signed by a U.S. citizen or permanent resident employed by the qualified employer on a permanent basis in an executive, managerial, or supervisory capacity for the prior year. File the petition with:

- evidence you:
  - maintain an established international cultural exchange program;
  - have designated a qualified employee to administer the program and serve as liaison with INS;
  - have been doing business in the U.S. for the past two years;
  - will offer the alien wages and working conditions comparable to those accorded local domestic workers similarly employed;
  - employ at least 5 full)time U.S. citizen or permanent resident workers
  - have the financial ability to remunerate the participant(s), as shown by your most recent annual report, business income tax return, or other form of certified accountant's report;
- catalogs, brochures or other types of material which illustrate that:
  - the cultural component is designed to give a overview of the attitude, customs, history, heritage, philosophy, tradition, and/or other cultural attributes of the participant's home country;
  - the employment or training takes place in a public setting where the sharing of the culture of their country of nationality can be achieved through direct interaction with the American public; and

- the American public will derive an obvious cultural benefit from the program.

However, if the proposed dates of employment are within 15 months of the approval of a prior "Q" petition filed by you for the same international cultural exchange program, and that earlier petition was filed with the above evidence of the program, you may submit a copy of the approval notice for that prior petition in lieu of the evidence about the program required above.

▸ **Petition only required for alien in the U.S. to change status or extend stay:** The following classifications do not require a petition for new employment if the alien is outside the U.S. The alien should instead contact a U.S. Consulate for information about a visa or admission. Use this form to petition for a change of status, concurrent employment, or an extension of stay.

A petition for change of status to one of the classifications described in this part must be filed with the initial evidence listed below and with the initial evidence required by the separate instructions for all petitions involving change of status. A petition for an extension of stay must be filed with the initial evidence listed below and with the initial evidence required by the separate instructions for all petitions for extension. However, a petition for an extension based on unchanged, previously approved employment need only be filed with the the initial evidence required by the separate extension of stay instructions.

E-1. An E-1 is a national of a country with which the U.S. has a treaty of friendship, commerce, and navigation who is coming to the U.S. to engage in substantial trade between the U.S. and the alien's country of nationality. Substantial trade means that your trading activities with the U.S. comprise more than 50% of your total volume of business transactions in the U.S. and that there is a continued course of international trade.

E-2. An E-2 is a national of a country with which the U.S. has a bilateral investment treaty or agreement, who is coming to the U.S. to direct and develop the operations of an enterprise in which he/she has invested or is in the process of investing substantially. A substantial investment is one in which personal funds or assets are put at risk in a real operating enterprise which generates services or goods. You must show that you are able to direct and develop the enterprise by having control over the business. You must also show that the investment is not your main source of income or that the proceeds from the investment are significantly greater than a subsistence income.

An **E-1** or **E-2** may also be an employee of a qualified treaty alien or treaty company. If so, the alien must be an executive or manager, an individual with specialized qualifications that are essential to the efficient operation of the employer's business enterprise, a highly trained technician, or start-up personnel (E-2 only).

E Petition requirements. A principal treaty trader or investor or the qualified employer may file the petition. It must be filed with copies of evidence of:
- ownership and nationality, including lists of investors with current status and nationality, stock certificates, certificates of ownership issued by the commercial section of a foreign embassy, and reports from a certified professional accountant (CPA);
- substantial trade if filing for an E-1, including copies of three or more of the following: bills of lading, customs receipts, letters of credit, insurance papers documenting commodities imported, purchase orders, carrier inventories, trade brochures, sales contracts.
- substantial investment if filing for an E-2, including copies of partnership agreements (with a statement on proportionate ownership), articles of incorporation, payments for the rental of business premises or office equipment, business licenses, stock certificates, office inventories (goods and equipment purchased for the business), insurance appraisals, advertising invoices, annual reports, net worth statements from certified professional accountants, business bank accounts containing funds for routine operations, funds held in escrow;

- if filing for an employee, evidence he/she is a manager or executive, or evidence of special knowledge, skills, training, or education, such as certificates, diplomas or transcripts, letters from employers describing job titles, duties, and the level of education and knowledge required, operators' manuals, and for non-executive/managerial employees, evidence that qualified U.S. workers are not available.

R-1. An R-1 is an alien who, for at least 2 years, has been a member of a religious denomination having a bona fide nonprofit, religious organization in the U.S., coming temporarily to work solely:
- as a minister of that denomination,
- in a professional capacity in a religious vocation or occupation for that organization, or
- in a religious vocation or occupation for the organization or its nonprofit affiliate.

The petition must be filed by a U.S. employer with:
- a letter from the authorizing official of the religious organization establishing that the proposed services and alien qualify above;
- a letter or letters from the authorizing officials of the religious denomination or organization attesting to the alien's membership in the religious denomination explaining, in detail, the person's religious work and all employment during the past 2 years and the proposed employment; and
- a copy of the tax-exempt certificate showing the religious organization, and any affiliate which will employ the person, is a bona fide nonprofit, religious organization in the U.S. and is exempt from taxation in accordance with section 501(c)(3) of the Internal Revenue Code of 1986;

TC. A TC is a Canadian citizen coming to the U.S. temporarily under the provisions of the United States-Canada Free-Trade Agreement. A U.S. employer or a foreign employer may file the petition. File the petition with:
- a letter stating the activity to be engaged in, the purpose of entry, the anticipated length of stay, and the arrangements for remuneration; and
- evidence the alien meets the educational and/or licensing requirements for the profession or occupation.

Change of status.

In addition to the initial evidence for the classification you are requesting, a petition requesting a change of status for an alien in the U.S. must be filed with a copy of the Form I-94, Nonimmigrant Arrival/Departure Record, of the employee(s). [Family members should use Form I-539 to apply for a change of status.] A nonimmigrant who must have a passport to be admitted must keep that passport valid during his/her entire stay. If a required passport is not valid, file a full explanation with your petition.

The following are **not eligible** to change status:
- an alien admitted under a visa waiver program;
- an alien in transit (C) or in transit without a visa (TWOV);
- a crewman (D);
- a fiance(e) or his/her dependent (K);
- a J-1 exchange visitor whose status was for the purpose of receiving graduate medical training;
- a J-1 exchange visitor subject to the foreign residence requirement who has not received a waiver of that requirement;
- an M-1 student to an H classification if training received as an M-1 helped him/her qualify for H classification.

Extension of stay.

A petition requesting an extension of stay for an employee in the U.S. must be filed with a copy of the Form I-94, Nonimmigrant Arrival/Departure Record, of the employee(s), and a letter from the petitioner explaining the reasons for the extension. [Family members should use Form I-539 to file for an extension of stay.] A nonimmigrant who must have a passport to be admitted must keep that passport valid during his/her entire stay. If a required passport is not valid, file a full explanation with your petition. Where there has been a change in the circumstances of employment, also submit the evidence required for a new petition.

Where there has been no change in the circumstances of employment, file your petition with the appropriate supplement and with your letter describing the continuing employment, and:

- if for H-1A status, submit a current copy of the Department of Labor's notice of acceptance of the petitioner's attestation.
- if for H-1B status, submit an approved labor condition application for the specialty occupation valid for the period of time requested.
- if for H-2B status, submit a labor certification valid for the dates of the extension.
- if for H-2A status, submit a labor certification valid for the dates of the extension unless it is based on a continuation of employment authorized by the approval of a previous petition filed with a certification and the extension will last no longer than the previously authorized employment and no longer than 2 weeks.

General Evidence.

Written consultation. Noted classifications require a written consultation with a recognized peer group, union, and/or management organization regarding the nature of the work to be done and the alien's qualifications before the petition may be approved. To obtain timely adjudication of a petition, you should obtain a written advisory opinion from an appropriate peer group, union, and/or management organization and submit it with the petition.

If you file a petition without the advisory opinion, it is advisable for you to send a copy of the petition and all supporting documents to the appropriate organization when you file the petition with INS, and indicate in the petition which organization you sent it to. Explain to the organization that they will be contacted by INS for an advisory opinion. If an accepted organization does not issue an advisory opinion within a given time period, a decision will be made based upon the evidence of record. If you do not know the name of an appropriate organization with which to consult, please indicate so on the petition. However, it will require a substantially longer period to process a petition filed without the actual advisory opinion.

Translations. Any foreign language document must be accompanied by a full English translation which the translator has certified as complete and correct, and by the translator's certification that he or she is competent to translate from the foreign language into English.

Copies. If these instructions state that a copy of a document may be filed with this petition, and you choose to send us the original, we may keep that original for our records.

H-1B and H-2B Notice.

The Immigration and Nationality Act makes a petitioner liable for the reasonable cost of return transportation for an H-1B or H-2B alien who is dismissed before the end of the authorized employment.

When To File.

File your petition as soon as possible, but no more than 4 months before the proposed employment will begin or the extension of stay is required. If you do not submit your petition at least 45 days before the employment will begin, petition processing, and subsequent visa issuance, may not be completed before the alien's services are required or previous employment authorization ends.

Where to File.

Mail this petition to the appropriate INS Service Center, except that:

- if the person is applying for admission as an L-1 under the U.S.-Canada Free Trade Agreement, the petition may be filed at the port of entry when the person applies for entry;
- if the services or training will be solely in Guam or the Virgin Islands, file the petition at the local INS office there.

In any other instance, mail this petition to the Service Center indicated below. If the services or training will be in more than one place, mail the petition to the Service Center with jurisdiction over the first work or training site. A blanket L petition should be mailed to the Service center with jurisdiction over the petitioner's location.

If the work or training will be in:
Alabama, Connecticut, Delaware, District of Columbia, Florida, Georgia, Maine, Maryland, Massachusetts, New Hampshire, New Jersey, New York, North Carolina, Pennsylvania, Puerto Rico, Rhode Island, South Carolina, Vermont, Virginia, or West Virginia; mail your petition to USINS, Eastern Service Center, 75 Lower Welden Street, St. Albans, VT 05479-0001.

If the work or training will be in:
Arizona, California, Hawaii, or Nevada; mail your petition to USINS, Western Service Center, P.O. Box 30040, Laguna Niguel, CA 92607-0040.

If the work or training will be elsewhere in the United States; mail your petition to USINS Northern Service Center, 100 Centennial Mall North, Room, B-26, Lincoln, NE 68508.

Fee.

The fee for this petition is a base fee of $70.00 + either:

- $10 per worker if you are requesting consulate or POE notification for visa issuance or admission [block (a) in Part 2, Question 4]; or
- $80 per worker if requesting a change of status [block (b) in Part 2, Question 4]; or
- $50 per worker if requesting an extension of stay [block (c) in Part 2, Question 4].

The fee must be submitted in the exact amount. It cannot be refunded. DO NOT MAIL CASH. All checks and money orders must be drawn on a bank or other institution located in the United States and must be payable in United States currency. The check or money order should be made payable to the Immigration and Naturalization Service, except that:

- If you live in Guam, and are filing this application in Guam, make your check or money order payable to the "Treasurer, Guam."
- If you live in the Virgin Islands, and are filing this application in the Virgin Islands, make your check or money order payable to the "Commissioner of Finance of the Virgin Islands."

Checks are accepted subject to collection. An uncollected check will render the application and any document issued invalid. A charge of $5.00 will be imposed if a check in payment of a fee is not honored by the bank on which it is drawn.

Processing Information.

Acceptance. Any petition that is not signed, or is not accompanied by the correct fee, will be rejected with a notice that the petition is deficient. You may correct the deficiency and resubmit the petition. A petition is not considered properly filed until accepted by the Service.

Initial processing. Once a petition has been accepted, it will be checked for completeness, including submission of the required initial evidence. If you do not completely fill out the form, or file if without required initial evidence, you will not establish a basis for eligibility, and we may deny your petition.

Requests for more information or interview. We may request more information or evidence, or we may request that you appear at an INS office for an interview. We may also request that you submit the originals of any copy. We will return these originals when they are no longer required.

Decision. The decision on a petition involves separate determinations of whether you have established that the alien is eligible for the requested classification based on the proposed employment, and whether he or she is eligible for any requested change of status or extension of stay. You will be notified of the decision in writing.

Penalties.

If you knowingly and willfully falsify or conceal a material fact or submit a false document with this request, we will deny the benefit you are filing for, and may deny any other immigration benefit. In addition, you will face severe penalties provided by law, and may be subject to criminal prosecution.

Privacy Act Notice.

We ask for the information on this form, and associated evidence, to determine if you have established eligibility for the immigration benefit you are filing for. Our legal right to ask for this information is in 8 USC 1154, 1184 and 1258. We may provide this information to other government agencies. Failure to provide this information, and any requested evidence, may delay a final decision or result in denial of your request.

Paperwork Reduction Act Notice.

We try to create forms and instructions that are accurate, can be easily understood, and which impose the least possible burden on you to provide us with information. Often this is difficult because some immigration laws are very complex. The estimated average time to complete and file this application is as follows: (1) 30 minutes to learn about the law and form; (2) 25 minutes to complete the form; and (3) 60 minutes to assemble and file the petition; for a total estimated average of 115 minutes per petition. If you have comments regarding the accuracy of this estimate, or suggestions for making this form simpler, you can write to both the Immigration and Naturalization Service, 425 I Street, N.W., Room 5304, Washington, D.C. 20536; and the Office of Management and Budget, Paperwork Reduction Project, OMB No. 1115-0168, Washington, D.C. 20503.

U.S. Department of Justice

Immigration and Naturalization Service

Please Read Instructions on Page 2

Certificate of Eligibility for Nonimmigrant (F-1) Student Status - For Academic and Language Students

OMB No. 1115–0051

Page 1

This page must be completed and signed in the U.S. by a designated school official.

1.

Family Name (surname)

First (given) name (do not enter middle name)

Country of birth	Date of birth (mo./day/year)

Country of citizenship	Admission number (Complete if known)

For Immigration Official Use

Visa issuing post	Date Visa issued

Reinstated, extension granted to:

2. School (school district) name

School official to be notified of student's arrival in U.S. (Name and Title)

School address (include zip code)

School code (including 3-digit suffix, if any) and approval date

_____ 214F _____ approved on _____

3. This certificate is issued to the student named above for:

(Check and fill out as appropriate)

a. ☐ Initial attendance at this school.

b. ☐ Continued attendance at this school.

c. ☐ School transfer.

Transferred from _____.

d. ☐ Use by dependents for entering the United States.

e. ☐ Other _____.

4. Level of education the student is pursuing or will pursue in the United States:

(check only one)

a. ☐ Primary   e. ☐ Master's

b. ☐ Secondary   f. ☐ Doctorate

c. ☐ Associate   g. ☐ Language training

d. ☐ Bachelor's   h. ☐ Other

5. The student named above has been accepted for a full course of study at this school, majoring in _____.

The student is expected to report to the school not later than (date) _____ and complete studies not later than (date) _____

The normal length of study is _____.

6. ☐ English proficiency is required.

☐ The student has the required English proficiency.

☐ The student is not yet proficient, English instructions will be given at the school.

☐ English proficiency is not required because _____

7. This school estimates the student's average costs for an academic term of _____ (up to 12) months to be:

a. Tuition and fees $ _____

b. Living expenses $ _____

c. Expenses of dependents $ _____

d. Other (specify): $ _____

Total $ _____

8. This school has information showing the following as the student's means of support, estimated for an academic term of _____ months (Use the same number of months given in item 7).

a. Student's personal funds $ _____

b. Funds from this school $ _____

(specify type) _____

c. Funds from another source $ _____

(specify type and source) _____

d. On-campus employment (if any) $ _____

Total $ _____

9. Remarks: _____

_____

_____

_____

_____

_____

_____

10. School Certification. I certify under penalty of perjury that all information provided above in items 1 through 8 was completed before I signed this form and is true and correct. I executed this form in the United States after review and evaluation in the United States by me or other officials of the school of the student's application, transcripts or other records of courses taken and proof of financial responsibility, which were received at the school prior to the execution of this form, the school has determined that the above named student's qualifications meet all standards for admission to the school, the student will be required to pursue a full course of study as defined by 8 CFR 214.2(f)(6). I am a designated official of the above named school and I am authorized to issue this form.

Signature of designated school official	Name of school official (print or type)	Title	Date issued	Place issued (city and state)

11. Student Certification. I have read and agreed to comply with the terms and conditions of my admission and those of any extension of stay as specified on page 2. I certify that all information provided on this form refers specifically to me and is true and correct to the best of my knowledge. I certify that I seek to enter or remain in the United States temporarily, and solely for the purpose of pursuing a full course of study at the school named on Page 1 of this form. I also authorize the named school to release any information from my records which is needed by the INS pursuant to 8 CFR 214.3(g) to determine my nonimmigrant status.

Signature of student	Name of student	Date

Signature of parent or guardian if student is under 18	Name of parent/guardian (Print or type)	Address(city)	(State or province)	(Country)	(Date)

Form I-20 A-B/I-20ID (Rev 04-27-88)N

For office use only
Microfilm Index Number

I-20 SCHOOL

Authority for collecting the information on this and related student forms is contained in 8 U.S.C. 1101 and 1184. The information solicited will be used by the Department of State and the Immigration and Naturalization Service to determine eligibility for the benefits requested.

INSTRUCTIONS TO DESIGNATED SCHOOL OFFICIALS

1. **The law provides severe penalties for knowingly and willfully falsifying or concealing a material fact, or using any false document in the submission of this form.** Designated school officials should consult regulations pertaining to the issuance of Form I-20 A-B at 8 CFR 214.3 (K) before completing this form. Failure to comply with these regulations may result in the withdrawal of the school approval for attendance by foreign students by the Immigration and Naturalization Service (8 CFR 214.4)

2. **ISSUANCE OF FORM I-20 A-B.** Designated school officials may issue a Form I-20 A-B to a student who fits into one of the following categories, if the student has been accepted for full-time attendance at the institution: a) a prospective F-1 nonimmigrant student, b) an F-1 transfer student, c) an F-1 student advancing to a higher educational level at the same institution, d) an out of status student seeking reinstatement. The form may also be issued to the dependent spouse or child of an F-1 student for securing entry into the United States.

When issuing a Form I-20 A-B, designated school officials should complete the student's admission number whenever possible to ensure proper data entry and record keeping.

3. **ENDORSEMENT OF PAGE 4 FOR REENTRY.** Designated school officials may endorse page 4 of the Form I-20 A-B for reentry if the student and/or the F-2 dependents is to leave the United States temporarily. This should be done only when the information on the Form I-20 remains unchanged. If there have been substantial changes in item 4, 5, 7, or 8, a new Form I-20 A-B should be issued.

4. **REPORTING REQUIREMENT.** Designated school official should always forward the top page of the Form I-20 A-B to the INS data processing center at P.O. Box 140, London, Kentucky 40741 for data entry except when the form is issued to an F-1 student for initial entry or reentry into the United States, or for reinstatement to student status. (Requests for reinstatement should be sent to the Immigration and Naturalization Service district office having jurisdiction over the student's temporary residence in this country.)

The INS data processing center will return this top page to the issuing school for disposal after data entry and microfilming.

5. **CERTIFICATION.** Designated school officials should certify on the bottom part of page 1 of this form that the Form I-20 A-B is completed and issued in accordance with the pertinent regulations. The designated school official should remove the carbon sheet from the completed and signed Form I-20 A-B before forwarding it to the student

6. **ADMISSION RECORDS.** Since the Immigration and Naturalization Service may request information concerning the student's immigration status for various reasons, designated school officials should retain all evidence which shows the scholastic ability and financial status on which admission was based until the school has reported the student's termination of studies to the Immigration and Naturalization Service.

INSTRUCTIONS TO STUDENTS

1. **Student Certification.** You should read everything on this page carefully and be sure that you understand the terms and conditions concerning your admission and stay in the United States as a nonimmigrant student before you sign the student certification on the bottom part of page 1. **The law provides severe penalties for knowingly and willfully falsifying or concealing a material fact, or using any false document in the submission of this form.**

2. **ADMISSION.** A nonimmigrant student may be admitted for duration of status. This means that you are authorized to stay in the United States for the entire length of time during which you are enrolled as a full-time stu-

dent in an educational program and any period of authorized practical training plus sixty days. While in the United States, you must maintain a valid foreign passport unless you are exempt from passport requirements.

You may continue from one educational level to another, such as progressing from high school to a bachelor's program or a bachelor's program to a master's program, etc., simply by invoking the procedures for school transfers

3. **SCHOOL.** For initial admission, you must attend the school specified on your visa. If you have a Form I-20 A-B from more than one school, it is important to have the name of the school you intend to attend specified on your visa by presenting a Form I-20 A-B from that school to the visa issuing consular officer. Failure to attend the specified school will result in the loss of your student status and subject you to deportation.

4. **REENTRY.** A nonimmigrant student may be readmitted after a temporary absence of five months or less from the United States, if the student is otherwise admissible. You may be readmitted by presenting a valid foreign passport, a valid visa, and either a new Form I-20 A-B or a page 4 of the Form I-20 A-B (the I-20 ID Copy) properly endorsed for reentry if the information on the I-20 form is current.

5. **TRANSFER.** A nonimmigrant student is permitted to transfer to a different school provided the transfer procedure is followed. To transfer school, you should first notify the school you are attending of the intent to transfer, then obtain a Form I-20 A-B from the school you intend to attend. Transfer will be effected only if you return the Form I-20 A-B to the designated school official within 15 days of beginning attendance at the new school. The designated school official will then report the transfer to the Immigration and Naturalization Service.

6. **EXTENSION OF STAY.** If you cannot complete the educational program after having been in student status for longer than the anticipated length of the program plus a grace period in a single educational level, or for more than eight consecutive years, you must apply for extension of stay. An application for extension of stay on a Form I-538 should be filed with the Immigration and Naturalization Service district office having jurisdiction over your school at least 15 days but no more than 60 days before the expiration of your authorized stay

7. **EMPLOYMENT.** As an F-1 student, you are not permitted to work off-campus or to engage in business without specific employment authorization. After your first year in F-1 student status, you may apply for employment authorization on Form I-538 based on financial needs arising after receiving student status, or the need to obtain practical training.

8. **Notice of Address.** If you move, you must submit a notice within 10 days of the change of address to the Immigration and Naturalization Service. (Form AR-11 is available at any INS office.)

9. **Arrival Departure.** When you leave the United States, you must surrender your Form I-94 Departure Record. Please see the back side of Form I-94 for detailed instructions. You do not have to turn in the I-94 if you are visiting Canada, Mexico, or adjacent islands other than Cuba for less than 30 days.

10. **Financial Support.** You must demonstrate that you are financially able to support yourself for the entire period of stay in the United States while pursuing a full course of study. You are required to attach documentary evidence of means of support.

11. **Authorization to Release Information by School.** To comply with requests from the United States Immigration & Naturalization Service for information concerning your immigration status, you are required to give authorization to the named school to release such information from your records. The school will provide the Service your name, country of birth, current address, and any other information on a regular basis or upon request

12. **Penalty.** To maintain your nonimmigrant student status, you must be enrolled as a full-time student at the school you are authorized to attend. You may engage in employment only when you have received permission to work. Failure to comply with these regulations will result in the loss of your student status and subject you to deportation.

IF YOU NEED MORE INFORMATION CONCERNING YOUR F-1 NONIMMIGRANT STUDENT STATUS AND THE RELATING IMMIGRATION PROCEDURES, PLEASE CONTACT EITHER YOUR FOREIGN STUDENT ADVISOR ON CAMPUS OR A NEARBY IMMIGRATION AND NATURALIZATION SERVICE OFFICE.

THIS PAGE, WHEN PROPERLY ENDORSED MAY BE USED FOR ENTRY OF THE SPOUSE AND CHILDREN OF AN F-1 STUDENT FOLLOWING TO JOIN THE STUDENT IN THE UNITED STATES OR FOR REENTRY OF THE STUDENT TO ATTEND THE SAME SCHOOL AFTER A TEMPORARY ABSENCE FROM THE UNITED STATES

For reentry of the student and/or the F-2 dependents (EACH CERTIFICATION SIGNATURE IS VALID FOR ONLY ONE YEAR.)

Signature of Designated School Official	Name of School Official (print or type)	Title	Date
Signature of Designated School Official	Name of School Official (print or type)	Title	Date
Signature of Designated School Official	Name of School Official (print or type)	Title	Date
Signature of Designated School Official	Name of School Official (print or type)	Title	Date
Signature of Designated School Official	Name of School Official (print or type)	Title	Date
Signature of Designated School Official	Name of School Official (print or type)	Title	Date

Dependent spouse and children of the F-1 student who are seeking entry/reentry to the U.S.

Name family (caps) first	Date of birth	Country of birth	Relationship to the F-1 student

Student Employment Authorization and other Records

Sphinx Self Help Law Books

Available from: Sphinx Publishing, P. O. Box 25, Clearwater, Florida 34617

National Titles

Debtors' Rights, A Legal Self-Help Manual — $12.95 [
Explains what your legal rights are when confronted by creditors and collection agencies.

Neighbor vs. Neighbor, Legal Rights of Neighbors in Dispute — $12.95 [
Explains all aspects of neighbor law including fences, trees, easements, encroachments.

How to File Your Own Bankruptcy (or How to Avoid It) 2nd Ed. With Forms — $19.95 [
Explains how bankruptcy works and how to file bankruptcy with or without an attorney.

How to Register a United States Trademark, 3rd Ed. With Forms — $14.95 [
Explains types of trademarks and step-by-step procedures for registration.

How to Register a United States Copyright, 3rd Ed. With Forms — $14.95 [
Explains what can and cannot be copyrighted and step-by-step procedures for registration.

U.S.A. Immigration Guide, Including the New Immigration Act — $19.95 [
Explains the immigration process, the types of Green Cards & Visas available and how to apply.

How to Draft Real Estate Contracts, 2nd Ed. With Forms — $11.95 [
Explains each clause used in real estate contracts and includes 5 different forms to save you money.

How to Draft Real Estate Leases, 2nd Ed. With Forms — $11.95 [
Explains each clause used in leases and includes five leases (residential, commercial and mini-storage).

Florida Titles

Traffic Tickets in Florida, With Forms — $14.95 [
Explains how to analyze your ticket to learn your defenses and options within the court system.

How to Start a Business in Florida, 2nd Ed. With Forms — $14.95 [
Explains Florida laws about fictitious names, licenses, trademarks, partnerships, unemployment compensation, sales tax, regulatory laws, federal taxes, and more.

How to Form a Simple Corporation in Florida, 2nd Ed. With Forms — $19.95 [
Explains advantages, disadvantages, types of corporations, start-up procedures, stock laws, etc.

How to File for Divorce in Florida, 2nd Ed. With Forms — $19.95 [
Explains Florida laws regarding divorce, property settlements and child custody and support, Includes forms for simplified and uncontested divorces and explains the procedures in simple language.

Landlords' Rights and Duties in Florida, 3rd Ed., With Forms & Caselaw — $19.95 [
Explains laws about evictions, security deposits, discrimination, abandoned property, housing codes, bad checks, residential and nonresidential tenancies, self-storage and mobile home parks.

Land Trusts in Florida, 3rd Ed. With Forms & Caselaw — $19.95 [
Explains how trusts can avoid probate, keep assets secret, avoid liability litigation. It also covers how to handle bad checks, residential and nonresidential tenancies, self-storage and mobile home parks.

Real Estate Agents' Rights and Duties in Florida, 2nd Ed. With Caselaw — $14.95 [
Explains brokers' and salesmens' rights and obligations regarding commission disputes, liability for misrepresentation, license suspensions and revocation, and much more.

How to Win in Small Claims Court in Florida, 3rd Ed. With Forms — $14.95 [
Explains how to file, settle, argue, defend your case and includes forms for claims, garnishment, etc.

How to Form a Nonprofit Corporation in Florida, 2nd Ed. With Forms — $14.95 [
Explains types of nonprofit corps., start-up procedures, charitable solicitation, tax exemptions, etc.

How to Make a Florida Will, 2nd Ed. With Forms — $9.95 [
Explains joint tenancy, homestead, spouses' rights, guardians, personal representatives, living wills, I/T/F bank accounts, and more, and includes 14 forms.

How to Modify Your Florida Divorce Judgment, With Forms — $19.95 [
Explains how to modify your divorce judgment, including alimony, child support, custody & visitation rights.

How to Change Your Name in Florida, With Forms — $9.95 [
Explains Florida laws regarding names and includes forms for changing name with or without court action.

To order use this form or call (800)-226-5291, (813)-587-0999 or Fax (813)-586-5088
Florida orders add sales tax. Shipping add $3.00 first book, 50¢ each add'l. book.

Name _____

Address _____

City, State _____ Zip _____

Subtotal: _____

Florida Sales Tax _____

Shipping: _____

Total enclosed: _____

Coming in September '92 Sphinx Publishing

How to File a Florida Construction Lien (and Collect!), With Forms $19.95 ☐
: Explains in simple language how Florida's Construction Lien Law can help you get paid.

How to File For Adoption in Florida, With Forms $14.95 ☐
: Explains in simple language how to file for adoption in Circuit Court in Florida.

How to File for Guardianship in Florida, With Forms $19.95 ☐
: Explains how guardianship works in Florida and how to handle one in court.

How to Probate an Estate in Florida, With Forms $19.95 ☐
: Explains how to probate a simple estate in Florida and includes necessary forms.

Useful Law Books from Nolo Press

Available from: Sphinx Publishing, P. O. Box 25, Clearwater, Florida 34617

Patent It Yourself, 3rd Ed. $34.95 ☐
: Explains every step of the patent process, complete legal guide for inventors.

How to Copyright Software, 3rd Ed. $39.95 ☐
: Explains just about everything that might be of interest to a software developer or publisher.

Plan Your Estate with a Living Trust $19.95 ☐
: Explains every significant aspect of estate planning, with specific instructions for preparing a living trust.

Power of Attorney Book, 3rd Ed. $19.95 ☐
: Explains who will take care of your affairs and make your financial and medical decisions if you can't.

Elder Care: A Consumer's Guide to Choosing and Financing Long-Term Care $14.95 ☐
: Explains how to choose and pay for long-term care. alerting you to practical concerns and explaining laws.

The Living Together Kit, 6th Ed. $17.95 ☐
: Provides information on estate planning, paternity agreements, living together agreements and buying real estate.

Simple Contracts for Personal Use $16.95 ☐
: Provides clearly written legal form contracts to: buy and sell property, borrow and lend money and more.

The Partnership Book, 3rd Ed $24.95 ☐
: Explains how to write an agreement covering contributions, wages, profit-sharing, buy-outs, death or retirement.

The Independent Paralegal's Handbook $19.95 ☐
: Explains how to go into business helping consumers prepare their own paperwork in routine legal matters.

How to Write a Business Plan, 3rd Ed. $17.95 ☐
: Explains how to write the business plan and loan package necessary to finance your business and make it work.

Legal Research, 2nd Ed. $14.95 ☐
: Provides easy-to-use, step-by-step instructions on how to find legal information.

Dog Law $12.95 ☐
: Provides a practical guide to the laws that affect dog owners and their neighbors.

Legal Guide for Lesbian and Gay Couples $14.95 ☐
: A practical guide covering living together, children, medical emergencies, estate planning and more.

Sexual Harassment on the Job $14.95 ☐
: A practical guide that explains the rights of employees that are sexually harassed.

To order use this form or call (800)-226-5291, (813)-587-0999 or Fax (813)-586-5088
Florida orders add sales tax. Shipping add $3.00 first book, 50¢ each add'l. book.

me _____   Subtotal: _____

dress _____   Florida Sales Tax _____

y, State _____ Zip _____   Shipping: _____

Total enclosed: _____

92   0684 241